Out of Australia

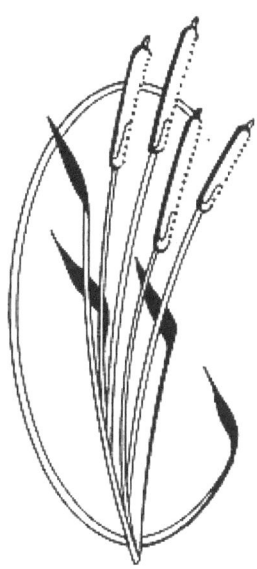

Out of Australia

by David J. Delaney

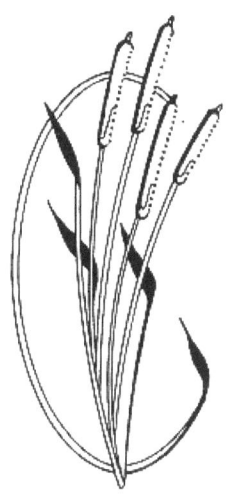

Proofreader
Elizabeth McCann

Editor
Shelby Jefferson

Senior Publisher
Steven Lawrence Hill Sr.

Awarded Publishing House
ASA Publishing Company

A Publisher Trademark Title page

ASA Publishing Company
Awarded Best Publisher for Quality Books

105 F. Front St., Suite 205, Monroe, Michigan 48161
www.asapublishingcompany.com

All Rights Reserved. No part of this publication may be reproduced, stored in a retrieval system or transmitted in any form or by any means electronic, mechanical, photocopying, recording or otherwise, without the prior written permission of the publisher. Author/writer rights to "Freedom of Speech" protected by and with the "1st Amendment" of the Constitution of the United States of America and the "Freedom of Expression" within the Australian Constitution. This is a work of non-fiction. Any resemblance to actual events, locales, person living or deceased is entirely coincidental if other than what is entailed within the boundaries of these poems. Names, places, and characters are within the work of non-fiction and its entirety is from a pictorial and written poetic autobiography and experience of its author.

Any and all vending sales and distribution not permitted without full book cover and this title page.

Copyrights©2011 David J Delaney, All Rights Reserved
Book: Out of Australia
Date Published: 08.09.2011
Edition 1 *Trade Paperback*
Book ASAPCID: 2380550
ISBN: 978-1-886528-01-7
Library of Congress Cataloging-in-Publication Data

This book was published in the United States of America.
State of Michigan

A Publisher Trademark Title page

Acknowledgements

The following Acknowledgements are for those, whom without their assistance 'Out of Australia' would never have been possible.

Firstly, to my darling wife and all family members, thank you for your continued support and love.

My good friend, Steven Lawrence Hill Sr. *President & CEO* of ASA Publishing Company for having the faith and confidence in my writing to publish this compilation.

Bernadette Curnuck for her brilliant and professional work on the cover of my book. bcurnuck@gmail.com

Hazel Menehira, Stuart Ross McCallum and Steven Lawrence Hill Sr. for their wonderful support and reviews.

I would like to thank all my friends at Tropical Writers Cairns for their critique, support and unwavering encouragement, also to my friends at Book Creators Circle, local radio, ABC Far North and 4CA AM radio for your continued support.

To all my 'website' friends world wide, (you know who you are) to many to mention, thank you all for your wonderful support, advise and encouragement.

Finally to my friends below who graciously supplied photos, thank from my heart.

    I.R.Stehbens.   *Mick O'Brien.*   *Jo Polglase.*   *Terry Cutting.*

Retired officers and wonderful friends, Lt. Col. Paul Murphy and Col. Graham Fleeton from Military History Tours for their unwavering historical advise, support and photos. http://www.militaryhistorytours.com.au

Thank you to all.

David J Delaney.

info@davidjdelaney.com

Introductory

Within this compilation I am offering my readers to journey with me and view the progression of my writing from my very early poems to my recent, also, as a different approach, you will read many of my poems 'as is', and as they have been published, basically quite a number are unaltered as when first written, and, as I was happy with the finished product at the time of completion.

The success of my poetry over the past years has been not only wonderful, but a humbling experience as well, I know some of my poems are not perfect, but then we don't live in a perfect world, though, to be able to touch someone and have them smile, cry or laugh, while they read my poems, is, perfect enough for me.

I feel a substantial amount of modern poetry has been shunned by the average person, because, unfortunately amongst many of our brilliant & wonderful academic writers, some have taken poetry to the point one almost needs a degree to dissect & understand the written piece, to me they are only seeking appraisal from their own.

I believe poetry should be easy to read, motivate, invigorate memories, enlighten the heart, bring forth feelings of sadness or joy, make one laugh or cry and project a lasting photo image story.

Stephen King once said, and, re-printed with Mr. Kings permission,

"If a reader needs a Thesaurus to understand the meaning of what you are trying to put across; you have lost them!"

I also believe the success I am having with my poetry is due to the fact I write for all, I write from the heart, I write simple so all can understand, I also know that with increasing understanding of the English vocabulary my poems will grow stronger, but I hope never to loose sight of how simplicity can touch so many.

Achievement and recognition come with hard work and, as with my poetry, each new piece is a milestone and a step further into the future, sure, some of my poems lack the vocabulary expertise of those far more experienced in writing poetry than I, but, my poetry seems to resonate with the average person who relates to and enjoys reading my writings, so, with this compilation, I hope you enjoy the journey you are about to embark.

David J Delaney.

Table of Contents

Australian bush poetry

2007

- The Land I Love 9
- Westwood Pub 10
- Our Land 11
- Christmas Creek 13
- Stockies Revenge 15

2008

- Drought 19
- Black Cockatoo 21
- It's good to be an Aussie 23
- Cradle Mountain 25
- The Outback Track 27
- Creek Camp Memories 29
- When Ever You Hear Me Say 31
- Creek Camp Morning 33
- Swagman's Tale 35
- Final Run 37
- In The Shadow of Ghosts 38
- A Farmer's Plight 40

2009

- Truck Driving Poet 45
- Echo's in the night 46
- Do They Understand 49
- 150 years young 50

A Drovers' Lament 52

Best stay away 54

Two Mothers 55

Undara 57

Travelling back 59

War related poetry

2007

Diggers 69

Those 2 Mischievous Boys 71

Villers-Bretonneux 73

Lonely Sniper 75

2008

Heroes Amongst Us 78

Taking of Beersheba 81

A Father's Loss 84

2009

Heroes of Gallipoli 87

Campfire Thoughts 89

An Old Vets Christmas 91

General poetry

2007

The Old Man 101

Wet Season 102

True North Queenslander 104

Nightmare of Love 105

Lost Love 106

Loving You 107

The Boys 108

I'm Sorry My Girls 110

My Time 111

My Life, My Love 112

My Mate 113

Loving Again 115

Old Sailor Dan 116

Cracker Night 119

When Autumn Comes Again 122

Rainforest Dreaming 124

The Surfer 126

Storm 128

I Love writing 130

No Worries 131

Old Pandanus tree 132

2008

Six Feet Tall 137

Voices 139

Cycle 141

Barnawartha 143

Closet Writer 145

Consuming Darkness 147

I was there 149

Untitled Love 150

Crying Souls 153

He lives in the tropics 155

2009

- Night Mistress 159
- Male Dilemma 161
- Black Weekend 2009 162
- Sharing some Tea 164
- Colours of Cairns 166
- Gone 167
- My Poetry 168
- Monster Crack 170
- Will there be Peace? 172
- Grandchildren 173
- Ocean Life 175
- Wild Life Angels 177

Sonnets

2009

- The Pauper's Friend 185
- A Stockman's Passing 186
- Snowy Mountain Blood 187
- Nature and War 188
- Why 189
- Visions of Love Lost 190

ABC Topical poems

2008

- Henry and Billy 199
- They come and they go 200
- It's just not Christmas cheer 201
- Christmas, I'm over it! 202

The haves, have not's and the in-betweens 203

2009

Aussie pride, Aussie shame 207

Troubled Times.. 208

Promises made, Hope revisited 209

Let's work together 210

Political promises, Political circus 211

Bad decisions, Critical consequences............................ 212

Deadly complacency, proud Muso's 213

Sign of the Times 214

Mystery, intrigue, heroes and villains 215

Bunnies or Babies... 216

Out of Australia

by David J. Delaney

"Don't let anyone bring you back to earth
Keep shooting for the stars"

David J Delaney ©

ASA Publishing Company

ASA Publishing Company

Australian bush poetry

ASA Publishing Company

ASA Publishing Company

Australian bush poetry

My foremost poetry 'love' is Australian bush poetry, as a child I would sneak away to read and be transported to another era by the greats, those like Henry Lawson, A B 'Banjo' Paterson, Barcroft Henry Thomas Boake, C J Dennis, Dorothea MacKellar, Harry Breaker Morant, Will Ogilvie, and many more have left a life lasting impression on me and my writing.

After I started writing my poetry I sought out later generation bush poets and via Australian Bush Poets Association began to read and then came into contact with many wonderful and helpful bards, the likes of Glenny Palmer, Merv 'the grey' Webster, Marco Gliori, Carol Heuchan, Ellis Campbell and so many more I could name have helped me in my continual journey to be a good Australian bush poet.

ASA Publishing Company

2007

ASA Publishing Company

ASA Publishing Company

The Land I Love

Lying on this river bank, looking through ghost gums
Listening to dragonflies with their melodious hums
Dipping they touch, making perfect water rings
While not far away, atop a tree, a Kookaburra sings.

The growling of a Koala overrides the Kooka`s sound
Thinks he's being threatened by a Dingo on the ground
Gentle breeze's blow as I lie here and think
Then a Bandicoot wanders down to have a drink.

Across the bank a Grevillea hangs low with weight
It's full of Galahs, cackling mate to mate
Honeyeaters buzzing 'round a tree, where they made a nest
Oh! So many creatures, I couldn't possibly name the rest.

You ask, "Would I ever leave & settle in the city"
No! No way! I love this, all be it hard and gritty
To roam this land Australia, in all it's pleasantry
My home, my love, my country and my serenity.

Inspiration from a trip I did to St. George western Queensland. I had some time to spare so I grabbed my blanket from my truck & lay down on the river bank & absorbed the surrounds.

Westwood Pub

There's a tiny little place a short drive west of Rocky
And the locals that live there always seem so jolly
Some houses, a pub, merely just a rail siding
Beware of a couple of dogs, they like biting

But to me the central point is the little old pub
Where trucks stop anytime for a cold beer and grub
And I must admit, when I had my truck, it's true
I stopped there more than once and had myself a few

The food and drink, not really what this pub is famous for
This piece of knowledge has been passed into truckie folk law
Before climbing those four steps, while dusting off your hat
One has to step around this big solid stony chap

There he is, a life size swagy, yes so true
You have to believe me; you know I wouldn't lie to you
The publican told me "It's from some market I got him"
Been here so long, to let him go now would be a sin

I said "He's been here such a long time, don't seem to be a worry"
"I wish I had a dollar" he said "every time someone said I'm sorry"
When leaving here at closing time, usually a bit under the weather
They miss a step and grab the swagy saying, "aren't you a nice fella"

Well it's been a long time now since I've been back to Westwood
So I'm hoping soon I get the chance, you know I surely would
To see the locals, the pub and under a tree the dogs are panting
But most of all, at the bottom of the steps, the swagy, he's standing.

Photo by Jo Polglase
email jopolglase@hotmail.com

Our Land

Sitting alone on this stretch of white sand.
Thinking about, the wonders of this great land.
Briefly interrupted from this gentle sea breeze.
Humorous lorikeets, somewhere in the trees.

I love so much this land I call home.
Anywhere in her vastness I like to roam.
Mountain ranges, cattle tracks and passes.
Rain forests, plains, deserts, and salt water marshes.

To head far north, where it's summer all year round.
Or travel south, where it's cold and snow abound.
From east to west, where there isn't any snow.
Into the desert center, where the "willy-willy's" blow.

I might stay awhile, do some work, lend a hand.
So I unload gear, from my humble little van.
I'll pitch my tent, set up camp in this quite shaded park.
Must trek over, pay the ranger, before it gets too dark.

I'll sleep well tonight, remembering where I have been.
My body feels at ease, with the wonders I have seen.
Here I am in my beach chair with drink in hand.
Resting at sunset, waves bubbling over the sand.

How long will I stay? A month, or two, or more.
I will pack up and move on, now that's for sure.
It's my itchy feet, and my heart, they let me know.
That anywhere in this land, I know I'm free to go.

Christmas Creek

Just feels so right lying under the stars tonight
Gums and pines, highlighted by the campfire light
I'm hypnotized by this wondrous night-time show
Looking, listening, there's more to come I know.

High in a tree, eyes glint from an old large owl
Also I hear the rustling of a nosey Bush Fowl
Glad we are here, this area seems such a treat
This piece of paradise named "Christmas Creek".

Sharing this campfire, my brother-in-law
Don't think he knows, that I do tend to snore
Our wives, no! They won't sleep out here at night
Scared some animal will wake them with a fright.

My two daughters now sound asleep in the tent
Collecting for the fire, their energy all but spent
In the morn, after breakfast we'll grab our hats
Tackle the walks and trails along these famous tracks.

Imagine their wonderment at the canopy of tall trees
Hoop pine, bloodwood, cedar, such a variety to be seen
Listening with amazement at Whipbird and Bowerbird
Also Lyrebird and Parrots, so many they have not heard.

Watch the crystal creek running over rocks so free
Glimpse a Spotted Quoll sitting on the branch of a tree
Then after all this walking, reaching a lookout so high
Gazing over green forest's to where ocean meets the sky.

Heading back to camp, listening to the birds singing
Stopping at a rock pool, hoping to see Platypus swim
Rustling of a Pademelon returns me to the fires light
Noticing a Marsupial Mouse as he scoots off in fright.

My brother-in-law is asleep; his swag's hood covers his hair
Looking to the stars, taking a deep breath of fresh clean air
Marveling at the contrasts of this land called home
Drifting into contented sleep knowing anywhere we can roam.

Stockies Revenge

A little pub in central Queensland, this I've mentioned before
The one, you know! With the stone swaggie standing at the door
My offsider and myself were there and settled for the night
Full of that famous tucker, enjoying a beer and feeling alright

Bounding through the doors and knocking over some stools
Two young stockies pushing each other and acting like fools
Len the publican says, "Oh! No! Not you pair of larrikins!
You better behave, I'll not put up with your shenanigans!"

Patrons drinking at the pub now reach a staggering ten
The young stockies still mucking about, closely watched by Len
One stockie says, "I have to go mate, watch my beer for a while"
So down to the toilet he goes, his mate, gives us a devious smile

Then off the stool and out the door, like a flash he shoots through
I hear Len mumble something like, "What's he bloody well up to"
We, not paying much attention watching music clips on the T.V.
On returning he's all happy like a little child all full of glee

Time has passed, beer was drunk and tall yarns were said
I'd had enough so I signalled all that I am off to bed
Settling in my trucks bunk, tucked away from the night chills
Thinking of those two lads making each other look like dills

'Tis a glorious autumn morning, a definite chill is in the air
A campfire's burning "Ya want a cuppa; I've some tea to spare"
Looking at the young stockie, the one who shot out the pub door
"Sure mate," I say, "I'll share your fire, what are friends for"

Sitting in the warming sun and enjoying a campfire brew
The other stockie stomps up, "No time for this, I'm shooting through"
Jumps into his truck, then off down the road at a good pace
His mate here takes a sip then a big cheeky grin comes to his face

Looking at me chuckling he says, "He will be back here in a mo"
"When I left the pub last night, turned the rigs round, didn't ya know?"
Having a good laugh, and me thinking how I didn't pick it
Now returning, his mate blowing the horn and raising his middle digit

Remembering many other times we met with this larrikin pair
Probably still stop at the pub, joking, driving poor Len to despair
I know for a fact these two wouldn't change their life for quids
Driving over these old beef roads, acting like two larrikin kids.

2008

ASA Publishing Company

Photo by Terry Cutting
Email: cadtc@dodo.com.au

Drought

*Dawn heralds a new day
Breezes blow the same way
Dust builds on the fence rail
Homestead's dirty and pale.*

Teasing clouds pass on by
Too dry even for a fly
Machinery caked in dust
Chains coated in rust.

Willy-willy's continuous swirl
More dust they do hurl
Bleached skeletons dot the paddocks
Dead gardens hold rusty mattocks.

Old cockey gone to the city
Not looking for any pity
In his flat eyeing the sky
Alone the old man does cry.

Dawn heralds a new day
Breezes blow the same way
Dust builds on the fence rail
Homestead's dirty and pale.

For his home he grieves
Banks, calling them thieves
His pleas they find boring
Forced out that terrible morning.

Finishing his last beer
Onto the bed that's near
Dreaming of a lush pasture
Drifting to the hereafter.

Who'll know he's passed away
He will be found one day
They'll think "another old man"
Knowing not his life was grand.

Dawn heralds a new day
Breezes blow the same way
Dust builds on the fence rail
Homestead's dirty and pale.

Black Cockatoo

Black silhouettes against clear blue sky
Oh! So high they seem to fly
Turning, showing their flashes of red
Now in a Gum where they've made their bed.

Adapting so well to the changes about
Be it torrential rain or long harsh drought
Fleeing bush fires that sweep the plain
Returning to their tree, starting again.

Their familiar screech, heard for miles around
Dozens flock together, pecking at the ground
On the side of the road, having a feed
Where a truck spilled some grain and seed.

I know some have made pets of them too
Don't know, if it's the right thing to do
Should stay in the bush, but that's my perception
Recuperating injured young, are an exception.

For these beautiful birds we call our own
When you visit, please don't damage their home
I salute these endearing creatures so true
This unique Australian, the **Black Cockatoo.**

It's good to be an Aussie

Late afternoon, I'm enjoying the purple-orange hue
See Dog down at the gate, so I whistle for my Blue
With a cold beer in my hand I take a few big swigs
Survey my patch thinking "Yep! I wouldn't be dead for quids".

Along a distant path there's tall gums I walk through
An area with electric grid's lights with a sudden flash of blue
With a grimace on my face I know it's not nice to do
They eat my plants and seed; I cull the odd cockatoo.

Dog is whinging again as he slowly walks past
He's hurt a muscle jumping fence's, but it won't last
Not much longer now he can rest and sleep
Once again he'll be helping round up the sheep.

Hear the cook scream, I know she's looking for me
Sliding off my chair, grab my beer down the path I flee
Hastily to me shed, that all Aussie boys need
Surrounded by ghost gums, catching all the breeze.

I enter my kingdom surveying my surrounds
Bits of timber, iron, car parts and odds abound
This is my shed I can hide quietly not to be found
Dog's at home, next to an engine block on the ground.

Walking to a corner, the one I know so well
Moving sheets of iron, retrieved from my neighbour's well
Revealing a good friend of mine, he's truly ridgy-didge
A reliable mate of time, me trusty old beer fridge.

I grab a coldie from the many and moving to the wall
Relieving myself playing hit and miss with ants upon the floor
Wiping hands on jeans, I pat the dog as I walk past
Turning round I take a swig from that cold amber glass.

ASA Publishing Company

Walking towards the door I grab my favorite chair
Fibbing to the missus "it's in the shed in need of dire repair"
Sitting near the entrance, looking into semi darkness
Thinking of smogged city folk, helpless in small apartments.

Dog pricks his ears, he knows full well that sound
I take another swig knowing this one's gunna hang around
So I won't elaborate, but I am sure you can get my drift
Something blokes do sitting alone, being able to let one lift.

Looking round my lot, I raise my glass and say cheers
What more could an Aussie boy need, but a few cold beers
Enjoy and work this outback homestead hand in hand
Sit in his shed with Dog, loving this vast and beautiful land.

Cradle Mountain

Hands wrapped round my hot cup of tea
Robyn and Bev, stirring; it's only us three
Surveying distant snow capped peaks
Across plains of button grass, deciduous beech.

Where small Bettong's and skink hide in daisy bush
Young King Billy pines, skyward they push
Snow Daisies, bluebells, milkmaids add colour
Gazing at the cradle, mesmerized in wonder.

Stepping into this misty, chilly morning
Leaving the warm cabin, girls still yawning
Outside the door, in grass to my right
Greeted by a pademelon, not afraid of my sight.

Munching on berries which fell to the ground
Dropped, from many endemic bushes abound
Turning, hopping away into tall thick grasses
Startled by a Black Currawong, how close it passes.

Three of us now walking a small rocky trail
Listening to Pink Robin, Golden Whistler, Grey Fantail
An orchestra of sound from these many passerines
Brilliant colourful plumage enhances vibrant scenes.

Snow Gum, Bottlebrush, Tea tree, Dwarf Pine
Spotted with luminous green moss, so delicate, so fine
Small icy streams bubble over mossy stones
Hollow logs where Pygmy Possums make homes.

Standing on shore's edge, beautiful Dove Lake
Breathing clean, crisp air, all our lungs could take
Pristine beauty like a never-ending fountain
Nature's empowering wonderment, Cradle Mountain.

Frozen in awe of this alpine like sight
Picture postcard perfect peaks of white
We will visit again this paradise serene
Speaking of majestic wonders, a must to be seen.

Photo by David J Delaney

The Outback Track

Black roads disappear into the distance
Left and right saltbush eeks out an existence
No rain here for years, not even a sign
So dry some locals say, "It's a crime"

Midday heat's oppressive, driving in scorching sun
Old truck has no air con. It's not much fun
Taking a chance, open all windows catching a breeze
Keeping a eye out, dreading a swarm of "bush bees"

Eagles glide in swirling thermals looking for their fill
Won't take long to find fresh Kangaroo road kill
A half metre "Frilly" sits atop a small mound of rocks
Making sure the road's clear before scooting across

Galahs and Cockatoos line edges of the long road
Picking grain and seed left by a road trains load
One can drive for hours along lonely inland track
Before you see any people, houses in the outback

In the distance we see billowing clouds of bull dust
Road train's coming, move over, slow down is a must
Acknowledging each other on our long range C.B.
How quickly, changes of landscape, to this we agree

Surrounded by saltbush a roadhouse comes into sight
Parking, having a brew and delicious country bite
Some driver's say it's raining up north, this I know is true
Be driving all night, beating rising rivers just to get through

Hours have past, sun's setting; it's starting to rain
Careful not to slide into the table drain
Spotlights on, now bull dust has turned to mud
Across the road a sow runs followed closely by her bub

Tomorrow while the sun's rising, I will be home in north Queensland
Where the rainforest meets the beach, I rest my weary feet in sand
Have a few days off, unwind, take a load off my back
Because, soon I will travel back down that outback track.

Photo by Ian Stehbens

Creek Camp Memories

When the hustle 'n' pace bogs you down,
through all this haze it appears so brown,
your life spark is all but diminished
exhausted now your work has finished.
replace that fire and restless feeling,
grab some beer and bottles of Riesling,
head to the bush; find a creek bank high,
pitch your tent 'neath clearing night sky.

Stacked wood now crackling 'n' burning,
on the hotplate, my steaks are turning,
resting, I start to really unwind
forgetting pressures; forgetting time.
Legs outstretched now slumped in this chair
breathing emission free, fresh clean air,
watched by a possum wide eyes bright,
illuminated by campfire light.

Serenaded by crickets singing
with millions of stars shimmering,
fires glowing shadows dance on ghost gums
while from a burrow a bilby runs.
an owl lifts its head to take a peek,
kooka's with young tucked sound asleep.
I'm mesmerized by the campfire glow,
hypnotized by the creeks gentle flow.

Would love to stay the rest of my life
instead of clanging and city strife,
all those cars and the thick choking smog,
prancing pink ladies with matching dog,
there's office robots and their glazed stare,
sealed lips, not a smile, they don't care
how do they live, how do they survive
in this daily routine nine to five.

As curlews retrieve me from my dream,
I spy two geckos on a fence beam,
bright lucent moon highlights a clouds edge,
diamond firetails in mistletoe hedge.
feeling tired can't stop my yawning,
new scenes will greet me with the morning.
snuggled in my swag and fast asleep,
now camped beside this beautiful creek.

Whenever You Hear Me Say

Here we are again my love,
shaded by this Gidgee tree,
on this cedar bench I made,
our place, where we love to be.

Courting Robins flit above,
how they sing a lovely tune.
Through wild flowers breezes blow,
carrying their sweet perfume.

Listen to the babbling creek,
meander its winding way.
Then you softly smile and nod
whenever you hear me say……

Here we are again my love,
our old homesteads, clean and warm,
though the front gate needs repair,
looking rusted, tired and worn.

Can you hear that distant crow
with its harking mournful cry,
the yard's in need of water,
now so brown and parched and dry.

You remember during droughts,
we would come down here to pray.
Then you softly smile and nod
whenever you hear me say……

Here we are again my love,
Grandsons, they're out ploughing seed,
Granddaughters' in the kitchen
busy cooking up a feed.

Your emerald eyes still sparkle,
like they did when we were young
then that day I said to you,
'Darling you're my only one'.

On this anniversary,
remember our special day.
Then you softly smile and nod
whenever you hear me say……

Here we are again my love,
Boys return from hours of toil
 hungry for some home cooked stew,
wash away the dusty soil.

Mia's calling 'Nan come in,
kettles ready for a brew',
'Micala's finished serving',
we'll be waiting just for you'.

You're gently blowing kisses,
placing Wattle on my grave.
Then you softly smile and nod.
Turn and slowly walk away.

Photo by Ian Stehbens

Creek Camp Morning

Now flocks of rowdy budgies stir us from our dream
they echo early morning with their noisy scream,
as nearby kookas join us with their tell tale call,
while natures music sings far from a city mall.

We breath the fresh new dawn emerging from our tent
and notice signs where roo's had searched for nourishment.
Upon the grass, dew's diamond droplets are abound,
as now the campfire casts a soft blue haze around.

Suspended mist now hovers just above the creek,
a sacred kingfisher has small fish in its beak,
some diamond firetails are now feeding their young two.
I stoke hot embers boiling billy for a brew.

The campfire spreads the smell of bacon and some eggs,
as two pied Currawongs, they watch on spindly legs.
While four pacific black ducks follow the creeks course,
we savor breakfast, topped with our tomato sauce.

A chilly morning greets, these thoughts, my wife she shares,
as fluffy kookaburras huddle in cute pairs
young wallabies edge closer to the campsite fire,
now venturing away watched closely by their sire.

Though won't take long for this great land of ours to warm,
now soon galahs, rosellas, to the trees they'll swarm,
Then ducks and fowls again inhabit waterways,
we'll throw a line, enjoy these peaceful lazy days.

From mountain peaks of snow where icy creeks still run,
To deserts bare, with bleached bones under burning sun,
astounding beauty everywhere can now be seen,
when touring our great land, and, live the Aussie dream.

Swagman's Tale

I picture him now walking outback roads
holed shoes rolled swag and dirty patched up coat.
His vivid memories to me he showed,
so in this book of mine, his tale I quote.

He talks about the wonders of the track
how often while he's walking, sings his song,
he treasures all that's carried on his back
avoiding bustling, noisy city throng.

He loves this freedom swears he'll not return,
again designing suburbs all so grand.
where miles of trees they fell then clear and burn,
then build their mansions on the barren land.

Consumed by wealth, their power and their greed
polluted air and deadly acid rains,
do banking giants care if you might bleed
they con with ease and baffle people's brains.

He's wandered years, this educated man
absorbing nature's forests, lakes or plains,
this college graduate who loves the land
the gouged raped land he always feels its pains.

He knows the beauty of a misty dawn
while camping on a foggy mountain top,
breathtaking scenes that just can't be out-worn,
while in the distance agile joeys hop.

Drink crystal water from the trickling stream
and not from plastic bottles that pollute.
To lie beneath the sparkling stars and dream
the beauty of the land one can't refute.

Wet season rains now giving life from drought
as rainbows cross what was once dusty land
for now our precious country leaves no doubt
we can't destroy this beauty that's so grand.

Now sitting closer, by his golden fire
we are as one in the Australian bush
While birds sing like a never ending choir
as burning branches now I poke and push.

His old black billy boils the water hot
he pours a cup of strong refreshing brew
sits back enjoys this isolated spot
then says he shares his fire with only few.

With morning he will pack and then move forth
he's moving from approaching winter cold
these days prefers the warmth of the far north
arthritic bones now take a painful hold.

He'll Never live in an old people's home
so sternly did he make this point to me
traversing this great land he'll always roam
while cooking damper, drinking billy tea.

Until that day beside an old ghost gum
his body lies beneath the clear blue skies
a life now ends its travels with the sun
and then, throughout the land his spirit flies.

Final Run

Another bug ends its life, when meeting my windscreen
while in this gradual morning light, wild life can now be seen
Diesel engine purring along this open, flat section
Humming its melodious song, rhythm in perfection.

Crimson Rosellas scoot past, as against a head wind I push
Hawks hunt lizard breakfast, hidden in the mass of saltbush
Paddocks now alive with our great grey kangaroo's
Young Joey's hop about, playing in three's and two's.

Brilliant blue sky, not a single cloud in sight
this day seems perfect, everything feels so right
Laughing when I spy beneath this morning sun
in a freshly ploughed field, emus falling, trying to run.

Wondrous Australian beauty, I've been honoured to experience
Rainforests, deserts, mountain ranges, captured with ebullience
View our unique animals, living, in their natural habitat
Amazing scenes will greet you on this lonely country track.

Staring in my mirror, now the road becomes the past
For a time I'll not drive again, as this trip will be my last
I know I'll miss the outback, the wide and sweeping plains
Caught with other drivers at flooded rivers during heavy rains.

Yes! I know it's true, now to spend time with my darling wife
Watch our grandchildren grow, help steer them from trouble and strife
Resurrect that vege. patch, clear the strangling brood
Resting in our patio, enjoying beer and home cooked food.

Though, I know late at night, when in my bed asleep
I'll be behind that wheel again, special memories to keep
Traversing over mountains, changing through those gears
Listening to that diesel engine, humming in my ears.

*Winner September 2008 "Poetry showcase" award from the
Creative Pen worldwide poetry site.*

ASA Publishing Company

In the Shadow of Ghosts

To all and sundry I hereby attest
when writing stories, I will pen my best
to literary heights I will aspire
and write like poets, those that I admire.

To stroll with Lawson under silver moon
and sit with Dennis in the early noon
ride with Morant along the Condamine
inspired by Parkes, my rhyme I will refine.

Then walk with Kendall, hear the bell birds song
stand with Ogilvie, view the rushing throng
watch Evans write his women of the west
read Boake, great poet and one of our best.

There's Esson's tribute to the shearer's wife.
the convicts who sang their rum song of life
then Song of Australia was Carleton's view
I hear Paterson, and that Geebung crew.

Verse caught the time, the man rode Snowy's side
viewed Sydney town when ships moved with the tide
rode Cobb and Co. along a dusty track
travelled the bush, where some never came back.

All master poets, experts in this craft
read so many, I smiled, I cried, I laughed
published in many a books well read pages
their words are still resounding through the ages.

I'll keep on writing well into the night
knowing one day, I'll pen the metre right
the flow of my rhythm will be like a song
the beat will sound its perfect soft and strong.

With help from writers, present or the past
my writings' true perfection, I will grasp
when all's left are my poems and my rhyme
I would love them remembered for all time.

A Farmer's Plight

Kicking the ground in despair
Breathing in dry dusty air
A lonely tear rolls down his face
How long can he survive in this place?

Surveying desolate barren ground
Grass, weeds, animals not to be found
Only the haunting cry of a single crow
Now hot winds are starting to blow.

Blowing to the homestead brown
White replaced by dust blown abound
Fly screen doors heavily caked
Water troughs, empty, cracked, baked.

Machinery stands idle in a shed
Payments so far behind, into the "red"
Banks don't care, want their money back
No chance of working into the "black".

Wife and children left, moved into town
Couldn't stay with such desolation around
Thinking of him she hopes he's fine
Then late at night for her, it's crying time.

Memories of great grandfather working this land
No more than a horse, plow and bare hands
In all weather from early morning light
Resting only, with coming of night.

Watching a shadow cross his eye
Speckled grey clouds pass on by
Falling to his knees, dusty ground now closer
Clasping a crumpled letter, banks foreclosure.

Demoralized! How many kicks will he receive?
Is this it? Can he get a reprieve?
One shot could finish it all now
Thinks of his family, alone in town.

Life's full of choices, some hard to comprehend
Does one "give up", just let it all end?
Stand and fight, be part of mankind
Gather yourself together, don't decide blind.

"A Farmer's Plight" awarded a Commended place in the 2008 Tasmanian Gumblossoms competition. Submitted and accepted for publication in "The Curious Record" edition # 21 a N.S.W. magazine distributed world wide.

2009

ASA Publishing Company

Truck Driving Poet

Goannas motionless in searing sun,
absorbing energy, life-giving rays.
Galahs, Cockatoos seek shade in a gum,
Bilbies in cool burrows these scorching days.

Hawks, Eagles ride summer thermals above,
heatwaves swirl in mesmerising dances.
A feral cat dines on a peaceful dove,
near road's edge a mulga snake advances.

Here I am on this old track once again,
my old rig's cruising at a gentle speed,
Engine's humming a steady R.P.M.
with stifling heat my sweat now runs in beads.

I'm keeping pace at ninety K's an hour,
no need for blowing tyres way out west,
one's energy, this temperature devours,
changing wheels in this heat I do detest.

It's been a good day, this long ten hour stint,
no 'Roos, Wallabies or Emus I've hit.
blinding afternoon sun now makes me squint,
my mouth's so dry, now I can't even spit.

Windows wide open for a slight reprieve,
This rig's too old for air conditioning.
I tell my stories but some disbelieve,
To publishers I keep propositioning.

Relieved as the roadhouse comes into view,
wash away the day, enjoy a cold beer.
In awe of evening's orange purple hue,
Write my poetry, the short time I'm here.

Echo's in the night

Autumn rain falling on my roof
disturbs me from my slumber,
I hear a distant truck approach,
twin stacks sounding like thunder.

In the darkness twenty-two wheels
now echo an eerie whine,
trying to close my sleep starved eyes,
drifting to another time.

A time when I was out there too
and mixing it with the best,
driving along a coastal road
Or hauling out to the west.

The only work I've ever known
now became my way of life
Certainly was made easier
with a very patient wife.

It's often said that life itself,
likes dealing a vicious blow,
deciding to take the "Putty",
almost produced a widow.

Now anyone who has driven
up or down the Putty range,
knows that your fate is in God's hands,
and how quickly life can change.

Soft rain was falling through the day,
felt like it would be all night,
my rig was feeling O. K,
and everything seemed alright.

From the radio Slim's singing,
while through darkness bull lights shone.
Remembering that final turn,
and how it all went wrong.

My rig was losing traction fast,
the whole truck began to slide,
fearing this is my last run,
we tumble over the side.

All media covered the scene,
clippings' are in my log book,
now and then I build up courage,
open it and take a look.

Two months in a deathly coma,
now lifetime medication.
No more cruising down the highway,
no lower body sensation.

Awoken from my sleep again,
for now the rain is teeming,
just like it did on the Putty,
when no one heard my screaming.

I struggle from my well used bed,
head off into the kitchen.
Boil the kettle for a cuppa,
some sugar now will sweeten.

I, driving different wheels these days,
still have chrome and leather seats,
With an added "ah-oogah" horn,
my wife thinks it's all quite neat.

Retreating to the patio,
in early darkness I sit
I hear a distant semi come.
This life, I slowly now submit.

Do They Understand

Do they understand, bout driving this great land?
Viewing rivers, plains and mountain ranges grand
Sleep beneath stars, that shimmer oh so bright
On a balmy crystal clear, peaceful summers night.
Watch our Kangaroos graze in morning sun
Along the open spaces, where our Emu's run
Or Budgies by the thousands, gathered round a water hole
The beautiful movements of a frisky new born foal.

Do they know, overpowering loneliness?
How late at night, you're haunted by the emptiness.
No longer a job, but an addictive way of life
The hurt, leaving behind your children and your wife.
Knowing how she lies there, restless with every sound
Agonises 'till she knows, that I am homeward bound
When we'll be together, albeit a short time
Then I'm gone again, following that long white line.

Do they care, sleeping in their beds so fine?
While we drive the night, to make a company deadline
Carrying goods, some for supermarket racks
Not thinking, of us truck driving insomniacs
They're first to complain, if we do something wrong
While they dawdle around, with the collard office throng
Then relaxing with family and all their creature comforts
Totally oblivious, to a truckie's tireless efforts.

150 years young

> Commissioned by the Cairns regional council to write and perform 150 years young at Gordonvale railway station on 25th June 2009 on the arrival of the Q150 steam train, celebrating Queensland's 150 year birthday.

We all acknowledge the Mallanburra tribe
your way of life has been transcribed
traditional owners of this local land
lived here, since Dreamtime began.

In 1859, we became a separate colony
forming our own Queensland state democracy
our population spread, west and north
to Queensland, many pioneers ventured forth.

Chinese "Coolies", some with wife hand in hand
worked the gold fields, then harvested the land
growing fruit and veg for the hungry city horde
fresh local produce that all could afford.

Priceless teachers assigned throughout the state
teaching children to read, write and calculate
often in conditions that would put anyone to the test
we should class all our teachers as simply the best.

Cane farmers, who worked from dawn to dusk
adjust to Queensland's way of life, this was a must
European families moving from trouble and strife
searching for a new home, a new chance at life.

For miners who toiled, extracting our precious mineral
their hard and dangerous work, is forever invaluable.
in unstable mine shafts, far underground
where the chance of a cave-in was all around.

Many general stores, were often run by females
as husbands tended crops or delivered needed mail
loading bags of wheat, or heavy bales of hay
these courageous young women, did it their way.

Drovers, walk a mob along a worn and dusty track
guided by whistling and the stockwhips echoing crack
traversing, long and barren dusty plains
or constant driving monsoonal season rains.

Timber cutters, for our state they'd sort, grade and cut
spotted gum, Red cedar, Silky oak or Blackbutt
supplying the needs of a growing population
sending tons to docks for increasing exportation.

Wharfie's at the docks, they'd ply their trade
working long hard days quite often underpaid
the tenacity to handle our bulging busy ports
with ever expanding, imports and exports.

We've travelled a long way in 150 years
shared a lot of heartache, blood sweat and tears
now our easy life style one just can't debate
it's great living in Queensland, the best Australian state.

A Drovers' Lament

Weeks he rides out on the plain,
a life from which he can't abstain.
Sets up camp amongst tall gums,
a clearing where the Cooper runs.

At the mob he takes a glance,
then see's two doves, who court and prance.
A large yellow belly leaps,
avoids a wedge tail as it sweeps.

Cockatoo's come in for a drink,
by the fire he starts to think.
Leans against this old Bloodwood tree,
remembers all her beauty.

Longs for her love every day,
little things she used to say.
The nights together they would spend,
thought their time could never end.

He had to go droving cattle,
for her this was a battle.
lonely nights she didn't foresee,
and moved back to the city.

His love for her he'd always show,
loved enough to let her go.
She's happy now with all her friends,
and the theatre she attends.

The camp fire sparks, crackles and spits
as the boiling water drips,
onto the flamed hot coals below,
as a breeze begins to blow.

Beneath this sparkling studded dome,
in the 'outback' he calls home.
Shares mountains and the trickling streams,
Now alone, he dreams his dreams.

Best stay away

Best stay away if this life scares you so,
the wild untamed outback.
From where a drought or beast can deal a blow
and sunsets take us back.
And then bright stars put on a wondrous show
while mesmerised we stare,
the city is a place we just won't go
it's where the throng don't care.

—

Best stay away from gloomy city life
the bustle of the street.
Where work takes us from family and wife,
then in a shop we meet
where we will dine the finest restaurant,
enjoying trams on track
and people push and yell and often rant.
You keep your wild outback.

—

Best stay away now why is this the call
we're living here as one,
as Aussies proudly standing straight and tall
when all is said and done.
Our Diggers died in far off foreign lands,
for freedom they did fight.
So you and yours can walk our golden sands,
enjoy an outback night.

Two Mothers

Ears spike then swivel on her head
there're twitching, listening for sound.
With eyes that search now overhead,
her hooves they stomp the solid ground.

She's drawing hard the morning air
now deathly fear is on display.
Her nostrils snort and then they flair,
while help now seems so far away.

Toward the house she runs at pace
for now she hugs the fence line straight,
as morning dew sprays from her face,
Continues to accelerate.

She stops now where two fences meet
while only meters from the house.
She calls, she paces and stomps her feet,
until, appear the man and spouse.

With words she just can't understand,
though, in her eyes they show great fear.
While trying to consol with hand,
is now a frantic Misses Grear.

So trotting forth from whence she came,
with concerned couple close behind.
now both Grear's fears, they can't contain,
and terrified of what they'll find.

Through foggy lower paddocks haze,
before their eyes the scene's unveiled.
Her first born foal of just five days,
there on a picket stands impaled.

Grief from both mothers one could see,
when both the females walked away.
Now down Grear's face her tears ran free,
thinks of another tragic day.

The foal was placed in clover green,
next to another smaller mound.
Both mothers now are often seen
their sadness shared without a sound.

This poem is about an actual incident, the only part not true is the referral to a human infant.

Photo by Undara larva tubes

Photo by Bev Delaney

Undara

New crystal droplets shimmer on gum leaves,
fresh smell of moisture in the air.
Life giving water absorbed by trees,
with birds and insects sounding musical flair.

Now Possums stir and wake from their tree home,
pink noses smell the seasons change.
Free from the heat they hunt and roam,
they seem to echo, chattery noisy exchange.

Mobs of kangaroos laze in the morning sun,
with paws that scratch then comb and preen.
Inside a pouch joeys suckle their Mum,
while they dine slowly on fresh grass cuisine.

Two geckos scoot along a thin damp branch
now they're watched by a kookaburra.
and fighting, there is a good chance
they will end up the kooka's breaky tucka!

Through palettes of colours view the vast Savannah sprawl
with stink trees, bottle trees and gums of white.
her captured beauty will always enthral,
each time you're taken on a special guided hike.

Along a boardwalk where the wildflowers beset,
now standing on a platform you stare in awe.
and visiting here you will never regret, 4
to all you'll share Undara from now and evermore.

You're feeling dwarfed by size the arching shape,
Undara's huge tubes are quite overpowering.
Through holes old vines and roots they drape,
while on-to ancient floor, sun's rays are showering.

now moving into darkness, intensified eeriness
as voices disappear well into the abyss.
and ankle deep water leaves you breathless,
the hypnotising beauty no person can dismiss.

It's always hard to imagine, so many years ago
when mother earth was young and changing,
that Undara had a great lava flow,
and left these massive molten tubes; so amazing.

It was truly a great honour and a wonderful time,
to visit Savannah with all its brilliance.
A trip to remember for a lifetime,
I loved the total Undara experience.

Photo by Ian Stehbens

Travelling back

My thoughts at times they stray
traversing this long track
Forget the time of day
and view our vast outback.

This old rig she holds tight
and always makes good time,
while Poets I recite,
they're helping with my rhyme.

I view the landscape's change
within this cabin warm,
from plains to mountain range
or through a thunderstorm.

How I would love to roam
just like our pioneers,
admire their scenes of home
throughout those early years.

I leave my sled of steel
with paint like sparkling gold.
Taut leather reins I feel,
I ride a dray of old.

As nature sings her song,
wild flowers sway with breeze.
Inside this billabong,
fish cruise through roots of trees.

To camp just where I like
beneath a shady tree.
A small warm fire I'll light,
then write some poetry.

Emerging from the glow
now shadows dance their dance.
A dome of stars on show,
I'm drifting in a trance.

I live this world today,
the rushing bustling race.
What would the old folk say —
they couldn't live this pace.

Photo by Ian Stehbens

"The poppy's might be wilted and trampled by the throng
but the memory of our fallen will live on and on and on"

David J Delaney ©

War related poetry

War related poetry

The heart tingling proud feeling and respect I have for our returned servicemen and women show through in the following poems and words just can't describe the feeling when I was notified of not only the inclusion of my poems in the International War Veterans Poetry Archives but also winning one of their major awards for my poem "Taking of Beersheba" and having my 2 line verse "Poppies" selected for their club theme project for the 90th anniversary of remembrance day.

Again, how proud I felt when I was informed my poem "Villers-Bretonneux" would be read at the post dawn service breakfast at the ANZAC day 90th anniversary commemorations from the town of Villers-Bretonneux. France.

Also my poem "Campfire thoughts" was featured in the Cairns Returned Serviceman's League's December 2009 "Sit-Rep" magazine.

ASA Publishing Company

2007

ASA Publishing Company

Diggers

Here I am, awake again, it's in the middle of the night
Lying covered in sweat, heart thumping from the fright
I truly wish they would pass and I no longer see
Nighttime in the jungle, another fight with the VC.

My wife is fast asleep; I know she shares my pain
I quietly move to the patio, and now it's starting to rain
The rain has a relaxing feeling, as I sip at my drink
I sit back in my chair, drifting back in time as I think.

Thinking of our old Diggers, returning from a campaign
Did they have the nightmares and unrelenting pain?
Then I know from any service, many are quiet and reserved
Shrugging away the recognition, we know they all deserve.

Serving in Europe, Asia, the Pacific or the African desert
Building a railway line, and in prison camps, did they deserve it
When they returned to their home, things seemed so strange
Did they get on with life; move on in their chosen game.

My memories will not fade, the mates who died in my arms
Or a group of us trying to cross those mine riddled farms
And the trip wires with grenades or poisoned bamboo
Booby-trapped rubber plantations, taking hours to get through.

These government experts, Ha! Put my memories in their head
People who wouldn't know, what it's like to crawl over the dead
They say it will be fine; I will get better and live a normal life
I know it will come easier with support from family and my wife.

And what about our young men and women Diggers of today
Serving their country, in a land somewhere so far away
All of us should support them, this we should show
Whether they are patrolling in the desert or the freezing snow.

So let's welcome these Diggers home, our arms open wide
And not like some of us, shun them, so away they hide
These young soldiers make me so proud I want to cheer
And I meet some at the RSL, and with them I share a beer.

I walk inside, my wife stirs and asks, "Am I alright"
Responding with "Yes" knowing it will be a long night
Feeling at ease laying here surrounded by these four walls
Thinking how wonderful it would be, a world without wars.

This tribute is for all our Diggers past and present especially for 2 mates (Vietnam), 2 Uncles (Korea), Father in law (WW2.POW Changi 3.5yrs), and a dear friend I worked with for several years who was a "Rat"(Tobruk). Also to other Diggers I have met over the years, their story's are and were amazing be they humorous or horrific.

Lest We Forget.

Those 2 Mischievous Boys

Well here I am again my friend, yes it's that time of the year
So, later I will wander down and for you I'll have a beer
But for now I will sit here, with my mate I hold so dear
And as with every time I talk to you, I know I'll shed a tear.

Remember the morn. We snuck into butcher Bob's from the back
Onto the floor, near the rear door, giggling we smeared some fat
Hiding behind some barrels, watching as he went "ker-splat!"
Laughing, running down the lane, Bob chasing, arms in a flap.

We grew tall and lean, our fathers proud, us, not backing from fright
Standing side by side, there for each other, even when in a fight
Our mateship people would say, was so strong and so tight
We would sort things out together, especially when we had a gripe.

Oh! We have grown together, sharing the laughter and the joys
Folks in this small town would say, "look at those 2 mischievous boys"

And women we had plenty, so for this my friend I thank you
You were like a "Valentino"; them giggling, you'd make them swoon
So at the dance we would always take one each home, it's true
Two young bachelors, no time for marriage, no, just no room.

You remember when the army recruitment bus drove into town
How we climbed on board, didn't hesitate, signed our names down
Then like two kids, all the way to my house we did bounce and bound
And how our excitement waned when Mum cried not making a sound.

Before we boarded the bus Dad hugged saying, "be safe, do it right"
Also if you could, at least every two weeks please try to write
We knew we had to do this, for people's freedom we would fight,
So waving goodbye, us two young blokes, disappearing out of sight.

Remember Puckapunyal, did our basic, we stuck together like glue
Knowing in these next coming months, together we'll get through
And at Lavarack Barracks in Townsville, from our town, just a few
A bit of time off, so down to "the nard" by the ocean that's so blue.

Oh! We have grown together, sharing the laughter and the joys
Folks in this small town would say, "look at those 2 mischievous boys"

Our last mission before we headed home. Yes, this our final one
Then VC start firing, so towards a fallen tree for cover we run
My knee, pain like I've never felt! Falling, now can't reach my gun.
Oh! The pain hurts so much, now thinking, will I see tomorrow's sun.

Our artillery boys, they start shelling from somewhere far away
Then our choppers and APC's come in and enter the fray
The medic, he reaches me and says "You're in for a hospital stay"
I finally look for my mate, not moving and so still where he lay.

So here I am again my friend, yes, it's that time of the year
And later, I will wander down, and for you I'll have a beer
But for now I will sit here, with my mate I hold so dear
Just as in every time I talk to you, I know I'll shed a tear.

Oh! We did grow together, shared the laughter and the joys
Folks in this small town used to say, "look at those 2 mischievous boys"

Photo by Col. Graham Fleeton (ret.) militaryhistorytours.com.au

Villers-Bretonneux

As we gather here this day on this historic occasion
Dignitaries, visitors and locals feeling heartfelt emotion
Remembering our Diggers repelling a ferocious German force
Helping to slow the advancing war, "history changing course"

Advance they did under darkness with typical larrikinism
These battle weary men, moving forward with precision
On the 25th of April, the Germans now encircled and trapped
Our Anzacs closed in, their energy all but sapped

The enemy, those not caught, bolted at a great pace
This town in ruins, devastation shown on the locals' face
Soon the rebuilding started, chateaux, churches and homes
The gratitude of these people, forever will be known

Saluting the thousands, for freedom they gave their life
In this time where oppressive and inhumane death was rife
To the 1200 brave young men who never returned
Their spirits in the vast fields, are forever interned

So for the beautiful people of Villers-Bretonneux
My heartfelt words I write for all, will be forever heard
Your thoughts and kindness in our minds leaves no doubt
That international mateship, yes! This is what it's about

To remember and honour our Anzacs every April as well
We acknowledge your suffering, at what seemed like hell
Working together side by side, rebuilding your town
Time has proved over the years, our friendship has no bounds

While back home, in the city or outback riding the fences
Those that returned, for a while forgetting the horror trenches
Remembering this town, and proudly wearing the slouched hat
Warmly referring to these wonderful folk simply as "Mate"

Now one thing that stands clear through all this ceremony
Something that can't be bought for any sum of money
Three simple words, prove our friendship will never be a failure
N'oublions jamais l'Australie or never forget Australia.

Lest we forget.

Lonely Sniper

As a child and growing in his youth, he was always alone
Through his teens, towards him no love was ever shown
An evil alcoholic mother, she really didn't give a damn
Father left when he was born, disappearing to some foreign land.

Fleeing his abuse to a rocky site high above the valley
Befriending an old Asian lady he simply calls Sally
Told him of her man and boys, roaming with the winds of ghosts
Soon the winds of time came and joining them, her free spirit floats.

Finally leaving home, tired of being bashed by strange men
Short years have past, he's still glad to be rid of them
Now under a bridge, laying on his roll by the fire's glow
What should he do with his life, which way he should go.

He always followed the winds of time, them leading the way
Whether chopping wood in a forest or fishing in the bay
Though something was always missing, something deep within
The wind spirits would show him, yes, they'll give their blessing.

A chilly breeze blows, brushing the side of his face
Again feeling lonely, missing Sally and their secret place
Blown from the grass, a newspaper page stops at his feet
Reading this old print, noticing a soldier, straight and neat.

Tossing and turning, on this long and chilly night
Knowing in the morning, he would sign up for the fight
Sign he did, not with the others but in a separate course
Passing with honours, proud to be part of this elite force.

Through his training, shunned, having no friends, not one
Spending hours alone practicing drill or just cleaning his gun
Transferred to another unit, taught the art of hiding himself
Enjoying this niche of the force, not working with anyone else.

Awake in his bunk, thinking of the tormented life he left behind
Tomorrow to be dropped in the jungle, beyond the enemy line
Remembering that night at the bridge, the breeze blowing around
Like an omen, the chilly wind taking him to where he is bound.

He feels he is being carried by the winds of time
Carrying him to ghosts past, singing their chilling rhyme
See himself being lifted, his body floating in the air
Waking with fright, now for his mission he starts to prepare.

By a large tree he buries his pack and parachute
Covering with leaves after tapping down soil with his boot
Settling on a high branch, a chameleon with eyes of a viper
In the darkness again feeling alone this highly trained sniper.

Morning sun behind him, ready, special rifle, silencer and scope
His target appears, soldiers reaching the top of the slope
Steely eyes are fixed, zeroed in on the general tyrant killer
A silent "doof", the murderous leader tumbles toward the river.

Soldiers that are left, start firing wildly into any tree
For a moment he lines up and shoots another three
Stopping for a second a familiar breeze blows across his face
A bullet piercing his chest, he slowly falls from his hiding place.

His dying thoughts are with the wind, he wants to roam
Lying on the ground his lifeless body cold and again alone
The breeze blows across his body taking his soul into the air
Joining ghostly spirits, now free to travel anywhere.

Sally said "Shouldn't be afraid to meet the ghosts at the end of life"
Only your body is buried never to suffer any more strife
The spirit is free, floating high, carried like a never-ending tide
Joining loved ones, travelling the universe so vast, so wide.

2008

ASA Publishing Company

Heroes Amongst Us

Sitting on this bench, my lunch I start to eat
Drawing nearer, wobbly cane, shuffling his feet
Stop's at a bin, starts rummaging through
Rubbish falls, finding his holey old shoes.

Moving along, now people step aside
Not knowing his pain, how many times he cried
Guiding their young away, thinking he's not well
Keeping their distance, offended by his pungent smell.

Long moth eaten coat, old canvas bag
Dirty beanie covers knotted hair, blue eyes so sad
Settles next to me like many times before
Asking, "You OK Ben, the leg still stiff and sore?"

We sat, talked for half hour or so
Ben said "Well time's for me to go"
Always struck me as well educated
Though at times appeared quite inebriated.

Prising himself to stand, slowly walks away
This routine, he's done almost every day
"See you tomorrow if that's OK with you."
He says, "Fine Sonny s' longs the sky's blue."

Thinking of my home, furniture and comforts abound
While this old man's content sleeping on the ground
Cardboard box warms him from windy night chills
Not interested in creams, lotions or pills.

Happy to live in his box of board
Meager possessions in his bag are stored
Old camping matt gives some support
Inner warmth comes from a bottle of old port.

Christmas day at the shelter, standing in line
Hearty meals served, he'd had a grand time
Home to his box for a good night's sleep
From the Salvo's a new coat, his to keep.

People's perceptions can be mean and narrow minded
On the homeless their comments, so misguided
Turning their backs on these unfortunate souls
Unconcerned at what past lives hold.

Again on the bench hoping for Ben to appear
Hearing some women talking quite near
"Haven't seen that grubby old man around
With any luck he's long left town."

Opening the paper, in bold print I read
"Another old man, yesterday found dead"
My body's feeling numb as I read on
Knowing it was Ben, not believing he was gone.

Police searched his lot, found in his bag
Historic memento's no one knew he had
A local reporter moved by Ben's plight
Wrote this article that very night.

Shiny medals, ribbons from campaigns past
Ben's story, finally told at last
Folded letters and a glorious citation
This man who unselfishly gave to this nation.

Saving four young boys from certain death
He alone destroyed a machine gun nest
Recovering in a field hospital bed
His tour over, with this mangled leg.

Unable to escape the horrors his mind bore
This man of men brought to his knees by war
Couldn't mould back into society
Wrestling inner demons alone, quietly.

ASA Publishing Company

Sitting on this bench, my lunch I start to eat
Drawing nearer an old hobo unsteady on his feet
Wondering how many like Ben are around
Living with their memories, sleeping on the ground.

Taking of Beersheba

What eleven crusades through history were unable to achieve
Nor' the victory, Napoleon had hoped to receive
Fifty thousand British fought bravely, alas they were forced back
Then Eight hundred Australian's took Beersheba, on horseback.

The world's youngest nation would now free the oldest
Beersheba, Jerusalem, Israel, fell to Aussie boldness
These brave boy volunteers from the vast outback
Wearing proudly that Emu feathered slouch hat.

Light horse infantry, not cavalry, as thought by some
Their qualifications; they could ride and shoot a gun
Many were younger than eighteen years of age
Accepted after lying on the application page.

Over four thousand troops protected Beersheba's line
Our boys had to go; even the horses knew t'was time
The attack was led by the fourth and twelfth light horse
They had to take Beersheba, there was no other course.

Bridles jingling with thirsty horses in jittery anticipation
Young men sitting tall in the saddle, the pride of our nation
Feet firmly placed in stirrups, they sat waiting for the call
To charge Beersheba, man and horse giving their all.

Starting at a trot, artillery formation onto open land
These horsemen with bayonets clenched firmly in hand
Tugging reins tight, now their horses' smelling water
Holding for the moment as yet this pace can't alter.

Echo's of "Charge", their "Walers" now galloping at pace
Adrenalin pumping riding, under fire in open space
Earth vibrating from consistent rumbling
Thousands of hooves, deafening, thundering.

Horses so swift, no need for spiked spur
Through bullets, smoke, n' smell of sulphur
Deadly shells exploding, deafening sound
Cascading shrapnel onto this bloodied holy ground.

British artillery now firing on Turkish defences
Pressing on they soon engage enemy trenches
Yelling n' screaming, including our Aussie coo-ee
Fearing defeat, the frightened Turkish they flee.

Four hundred year reign ended for Beersheba and Israel
God's hands were guiding, how could it fail?
Seemed like he had this battle already assessed
Genesis 12: "Those who bless Israel will be blessed".

History recorded, these eight hundred light horsemen
Taking Beersheba with a loss of thirty one countrymen
Their reputation through the holy land could not be matched
When reaching Jerusalem, the enemy retreated en masse.

New Zealand mounted rifles, British Yeomanry brigades
First, Third and Eleventh light horse, all deserve accolades
I know I can't acknowledge all involved in this campaign
So read their stories, accomplishments, trials and pain.

On ANZAC day, gathered beside this ancient well
Reliving 31st October, a proud story to tell
Heroic men of the Australian desert mounted corps
Your brave deeds remembered, forever in our thoughts.

When, is a battle's won, really a win?
Ask a soldier whose nightmares still live within
Or the heartbreak a mother feels when reading that letter
Knowing she has lost her dear son forever.

Our leaders sit, debate or preamble
Like the roll of dice, any campaign is a gamble
Nighttime in warm beds, away from wars strife
Are they truly remorseful, condemning a soldier's life.

Lest we Forget

Awarded November 22nd 2008

ASA Publishing Company

A Father's loss

How you've grown my son
Respected by our clan
Let me shake your hand
How you've grown.

How you're standing tall my son
Brass buttons shining bright
Leaving soon to join the fight
How you're standing tall.

How you march so fine my son
Rifle on your shoulder
Going where the weather's colder
How you march so fine.

How you stood waving my son
As the ship left the quay
Travelling across the open sea
How you stood waving.

How you sent letters my son
The stench of death abound
On that bloody battleground
How you sent letters.

Now you'll never return my son
Forever to remain over there
Entombed under French mud somewhere
Now you'll never return.

Inspired by the recent discovery of the Aussie Diggers mass graves on the former battle fields of France.

2009

ASA Publishing Company

Heroes of Gallipoli

The poppies might be wilted and trampled by the throng
But the memory of our fallen forever will live on
Their spirits free and roaming distant pebbled sand
Safe within the bosom of Mustafa's mother land.

Still can hear them marching, through the city to the quay
Fight for King and country, in a place that's called Gallipoli
These brave young Australians and volunteers by the score
Leave behind their loved ones to fight on a foreign shore.

Sailing far across the great expanse of sea
What's about to unfold, no one could foresee
Training for some time under Egypt's clear blue sky
Waiting for the orders to which they must comply.

Sunday the 25th a day that history recorded
ANZAC tenacity and valour so rightly was applauded
Turkish troops were ready, positioned themselves quite well
From their hilltop advantage, they gave our blokes hell.

Continuing to move forward with the enemy overhead
As our troops fell, the pebbled beaches turned to red
Some called it a battle; we know it was a slaughter
Many a brave man will never hold his son or daughter.

Nine months of fighting, with no strategic gain
Over eight thousand dead and many more in pain
They died fighting for freedom and democracy
Albeit by the hands of political diplomacy.

Evacuation was ordered; retreating slowly from that shore
Eleven nights it took, no loss of life was the score
Ever so quiet like actors in a pantomime
Most successful operation of the war, t'was regarded at the time.

That Sunday in April, the ANZAC legend was born
Now every year we pay tribute, salute and mourn
For these young men, called "The knights of Gallipoli"
You'll forever be remembered right throughout our history.

*"The poppies might be wilted and trampled by the throng
But the memory of our fallen will live on and on and on."*

Campfire Thoughts

Sitting by the campfire glow
do you drift in silent thought
think of diggers young and brave
and countries where they fought

Resting in their compound safe
did they stare at lucent flame
then imagine if they could
they were back home again

Fighting Boers in Africa
on the hills or open plains
did they circle late night fires
and miss their home town rains

Middle eastern deserts bare
under mesmerising stars,
did they stand around a fire
and talk of eastern bars

Near the battle fields of France
where so many gave their lives,
did they sit by warming fire
share photos of their wives

Once again in world war two
resting on Kokoda's track,
did our boys group round a fire
and think they'd not come back

Inside deathly prison camps
endless cruelty brave men bore
did the weak surround a fire
dream of Australia's shore

Hillsides bare, now in Korea
called the forgotten war
did our diggers make a fire
pray for their full withdraw

Troops were called upon again
now Vietnam's jungle dense
did they drink by campfire's glow
say, "this does not make sense"

Serving now on foreign shores
tropic nights or winter sun
do they sit by campfire warm
glad when their tour is done

Next time you're by campfire glow
drifting into silent thought
think of diggers young or old
remember why they fought

An Old Vets Christmas

He shuffles down a quiet darkened street,
alone, he always dreads this time of year,
cause locals, he just cannot bear to meet.
He eats collected scraps and drinks warm beer.

Now as the rain begins to softly fall
he crawls beneath a long deserted shop,
and hears the singing from the nearby hall
while all the time, he wishes, they would stop.

A flash sends goose bumps covering his skin
the sky now rumbles with a long deep tone,
then, brings back horrors hidden deep within,
again, he fronts the enemy alone.

Now mortars fall as with each lightning blast
he's foetal in his cardboard box and prays,
and shaking as his heart is pounding fast,
arms wrapped around his head, he rocks and sways.

He flinches and he moans with every burst,
relives the scenes held deep within his brain,
and wishes that the visions would disperse,
the sight of blown up bodies, still remain.

The rain's like thunder on this roof of tin,
like non-stop gunfire in a jungle dense.
He's once again a soldier in the din,
where many boys, lost all their innocence.

The 'war' is easing as the thunder dies,
he now releases clasping hands from ears,
remembers politicians and their lies
and how so many died throughout those years.

He hears again the Christmas Carols clear,
his shaking starts now slowly to decrease,
while in the darkness, sheds a lonely tear,
and knows that only death can bring release.

He'll fight no more this demon battle ground
as finally succumbed he starts to doze.
In time his lifeless body will be found.
This old man's story, scribes can now expose.

"Grasp life with all your strength
Because it's life that gives strength"

David J Delaney ©

General poetry

ASA Publishing Company

General poetry

The following collection of poems I 'loosely' class as general poetry, quite a number of these poems could easily come under the genre of 'bush' poetry because of the rhyme and metre structure, also a number of these ones are quite personal, and, whilst I found reasonably easy to write, I cannot perform some of these particular ones in public due to their nature.

2007

ASA Publishing Company

The Old Man

We are waiting at the steps, watching as the car comes through the gate
Everyone is early, taken their seats, nice to see no one was late
Around the drive and then under cover, it stops in front of us,
4 sons and 2 mates, yes we all know he did not want a fuss.

Then we lift him from this vehicle, this his final ride
We walk slowly up the steps; it's sad but also tinged with pride
Along the red carpet, past all the people by this isle either side
To carry him as he did us all those years by our side.

So to the end of the isle where we gently place him down
The mates and a brother take their seats hardly making a sound
Then us 3 still remaining unscrew and slide down the lid
For there are still some here, who, a final farewell they bid.

And as I see him there looking so peaceful and serene
No more pain, as in previous years I've seen
Oh! Yes we will miss him with every rising of the sun
Friends, Brothers and sisters, Wife, Daughters and sons.

I could write pages of stories of his love, hardships and pain
Only he would sternly say "don't make a fuss keep it simple and plain"
So this I will do for us who call him "The Old Man"
I will not harp or glorify or put him on a stand.

So we replace the lid and join the others with our eased hearts
The service was spoken, some sad but quite funny in parts
He was watching us there and at the wake thereafter
Yes, this was the day, our final goodbye, to our dear Father.

Photo by David J Delaney

Wet Season

I'm sitting in my patio enjoying another cold beer
Yes! Everyone knows, the animals as well, it's that time of year
Rain is falling in the tropics the wet is finally here

As I sit, I ponder at how it must have been in the past
And how our wet clothes, now, into the dryer we cast
For our pioneers to live through a wet surely was a task

It must have been an effort to walk in that red muddy goo
Or to scare off a small croc. Looking for a dry spot too
Too scavenge through the wood heap and find some dry ones "what a coo"

And a Mother and wife in the damp trying to knead dough
Trying to keep the young ones dry but typical boys, into the rain they go
They're there having a go living in this shack that they call home

I return to the present the water building in my back yard
Must place some agg. Pipe there shouldn't be that hard
Dig a trench cover the pipe with gravel, not yet, more rain is on the cards

I will have some work to do while there is a break, a temporary pass
The missus will be on my case to pick up the rubbish and clear the path
Until then I will sit here as I watch some birds through the rain they dart

The rain keeps pouring the roads are cut and towns are water bound
I envy people trapped in pubs the water rising around
All they can do is drink beer and listen to the rain thundering down

These my short thoughts and moments of sitting here in the wet
There will be many more reports on the news from the T.V. set
I grab another drink, and will I settle for few more beers, yes! I bet.

Photo by David J Delaney

TRUE NORTH QUEENSLANDER

To be here with all this rain is bliss
Monsoon magic, I would not miss
Mexicans who whinge and whine
Pack up, move back, double time

True North Queenslanders don't sit and cry
We love the wet, the rain, the rising tide
So what! For a while we move to a friend's
Later return to our flooded house and start again

That's what it's like living here in the north
Never a dull moment when the wet comes forth
Would I live anywhere else in this big land abound
Nah! A true North Queenslander, of this I'm proud

Nightmare of Love

Trying to open my eyes, don't want to pries them apart
My head is thumping, the nightclub it was so dark
She said she wanted me now, that's all I remember
Oh! That's right it's her birthday, this day in September.

I was so drunk, when I said, "You are the love of my life!"
Lying in this bed, what was that noise? It's not very nice
Oh! The smell, I can't move, your arm it's like a tree trunk
I'm going to die here, you're like the Titanic, and I think I'm sunk.

I struggle free, now I can't see, for my eyes are full of tears
You out of bed, I'm against the wall, why did I have all those beers
Stumbling towards me you trip, on the floor are your pantyhose
We crash against the wall, the pain, my god, now I've a broken nose.

Arms around me, like a big bear, saying you want me for your own
My head buried in your hairy armpit, and all I can do is groan
I'm feeling like an ant, trapped, in a soft blob of kneaded doe
Starting to lose consciousness, just wish you'd bloodywell let go.

You loosen your grip; I manage to slide out to one side
I grab my jeans and shirt, stuff the rest, as I dash for outside
You step on my jeans; we both go down and on the floor we hit
When you land on top, my head, now bleeding because of it.

My nose is bleeding as well as my head, I think my shoulder is broken
Ankle dislocation, cracked ribs, and not one word have I spoken
You're so big; I just can't believe it, a giant from a past life
So as I struggle to the door, you're yelling, "Make me your wife!"

I'm trying to run down the street with all the strength I can muster
A police car pulls up, they say "What the hell you doing buster?"
I tell the scene then plead, take me to hospital emergency near
Promising them never again, will I get so drunk drinking beer!

For a friend who used to work next door to me, this did happen to him.

ASA Publishing Company

Lost Love

A cold wind blows down behind my neck
It seems like yesterday we only just met
Now a lonely tear rolls down my face
Walking with my head down, at a slower pace

The sky has darkened, rain is starting to fall
My life is shattered, I feel like I've hit a wall
Gazing at this path as I walk, it's so pale and gray
Not knowing what to do since you left that day

The pain, like my heart's been run through with a knife
Should I continue, or just give up on this life
My tears flowed like a river, when they lowered the casket
To get through the coming days, can I get past it?

I miss you so much, god, only knows how it hurts
Back at our flat I try to pick up some clothes and shirts
Sitting on the bed, where our love was so wild
I'm crying again like an inconsolable child

Lying here on the bed looking into the dark
Why, why did your death, suddenly tear us apart
Going to be a long night listening to the rain
Because I know my love for you will never, never wane

LOVING YOU

Sitting on the bed's edge watching you sleep
You're so beautiful; I hang off every word you speak
Watch you lying there, knowing everything is all right
Also knowing to protect you I would give my life

Your breath is so soft, like an angels feather
Skin white, smooth, not yet aged by the weather
Hands and fingers like rose petals, so delicate
And with my mind I know you can manipulate

You stir, roll towards me, a smile upon your lips
Your hand reaches for mine, so gentle as it grips
Stirring again knowing you are close to waking
Or are you already and just lying there faking

Slightly opening one eye, your smile now wider
Fingers run up my arm, just like a small spider
Now on your knees, you give me a big hug
Through your hair, my fingers give a gentle rub

I'll stay long as I can to give you all my love
In life's journey, you will sparkle like the stars above
Grow to a wonderful person, just like my Daughter
Yes, you, my gorgeous lovely Grand/Daughter

The Boys

It's now morning, I hear them stirring, those two mischievous boys
Giggling as they leave their room, scattered with a myriad of toys
Softly up the hallway then scamper across the floor
They are now behind my lounge chair, I'll play this game for sure

I pass my cupper to my wife, watching and sitting in the other chair
Knowing what's going to happen soon, must pretend I'm scared
Then either side of the chair they jump up and at me they growl
I yell and then start to laugh as they roll around cackling with a howl

They are up now and sitting on each side of this big old chair
I put my arms around them and slide them to me, these fiery pair
Giving them a hug I hear those words that make me feel better
"Love you Granddad, love you forever and forever"

Sliding off me, they are so full of chatter
Over to the other chair, now climbing all over their Nanna
And growing with these boys it will be such fun, you see
Because more will be running around, as soon there will be three

And as he grows I know the other two will teach some of their traits
Like at mealtime, how to hide bits of food underneath their plates
Or hide under the bed giggling when their mum comes looking
And how to melt Nanna's heart when pretending they are sooking

But I see these young boys grow to be wonderful men one day
And often talk fondly of us, long after we have passed away
Their mum will be so proud of her boys, yes this is true
So until that day we will treasure hugs and the "I LOVE YOU'S"

I'm Sorry My Girls

Why, why did I do this throughout their young life?
Knowing at times it may have caused some strife
Was it because, as I grew up I copped the same
"Get up, stop crying, don't show emotion, play the game."

It hurts thinking that I wasn't there when they had fallen
Or to give a big hug, if a ankle or wrist was swollen
To be out on the road, it's like living another life
Guilty, things were so hard for them, also my wife.

Even today I find it hard to have a long conversation
Why can't I do it, why can't I hold this communication?
I so love these grown women, with children of their own
And often my silly feelings make me feel so alone.

Was I so bad a Father and Husband to them all
Often I would dwell on this until it drove me up the wall
My family never had that hugging, kissing type love
Dad and Mum loved us, but their kind of way it was done.

So how do I tell my girls I love them and love them so
When I find this so hard, not wanting to put on a show
The time I know when I should say "I love you, I do"
Instead all I can muster is "Till next time I see you".

I love them so much, it really hurts my heart
Sitting in my chair, thinking how far we are apart
One day soon I'll show I'm not that tough
To hug, squeeze, love you, and not be so gruff.

So I hope one day they both will read this poem
The expression on their faces, will leave them glowing
I love you two, love you so much, you see
To know before I go, your Father, I'm so proud to be.

MY TIME

Well, I knew this day, it had to come a round
So many here, all quiet and not making a sound
All my friends and relatives, some traveling from afar
Also down the back, having to hold the doors ajar

Wife, daughters and grandchildren, are at the front I see
Wonderful children, I know forever they'll remember me
Everyone around, why, why are they looking so sad
They should know, my life was full and not that bad

It was good with some disappointments, I have no regrets
To finally be here, at the end of this life of steps
I try to tell them my spirit is free, I have no more pain
But I realize they can't hear me, my efforts are in vain

So I listen to the service and stories told about me
And to hear all the kind words, it's a pleasure to see
As my casket moves towards the curtains, ever closer
I now see my father, he is waving for me to crossover

Feeling so at ease, my body and steps are so much lighter
Floating to the bright light, guiding me to the hereafter
So taking one last look at this wonderful congregation
I believe they know the place I go is of peace and inner sanction

My Life, My love

The morning light breaks into our bedroom.
And I know you won't be wakening too soon.
Seeing you lying there, so lovely and peaceful.
Perusing your sleeping body, oh! so beautiful.

I gently kiss you on the shoulder, I love you so much.
Running my hand down your arm, it's so soft to touch.
Fingers now reaching your face so warm and wonderful.
Thinking of last night, you're loving, so remarkable.

Feeling so soft, your hair running over my finger.
Your fast asleep, I'm thinking I can't linger.
So I slide off the bed, not making a peep.
I love you so much; I leave you to your beauty sleep.

Walking to the kitchen, my drowsiness starting to abate.
Opening the cupboard, I grab a cup and plate.
I make some toast; spread marmalade for you to see.
Boil the kettle and pour your favourite cup of tea.

Placing all on a tray, I return to our room where you lay.
You're still fast asleep, dreaming of somewhere far away.
The tray's on the bedside, on your cheek I give a kiss.
You slowly open your eyes, softly saying, "What's this?"

"Nothing special my love", the one I love so dear.
I am so happy it's just you and me that are here.
I say, "I love you, this day and for the rest of our life".
All this time, all these years, you my darling wife.

MY MATE

I remember I lost a good mate some time ago.
It was so dam hard to give the nod to let him go.
Then brought him home to a spot I knew he would like.
Placing him in the ground was a wrenching sight.

Burning his name on a post, before it got too dark.
It will last a long time, this remembrance mark.
Remember, I sure will, the words that he heeded.
And when it hurt me inside, when discipline was needed.

All the games we would play, oh! So much fun.
A walk down to the park, or a good long run.
Or when he wasn't looking, I'd hide in tall grass.
Hearing him circling until he pounced, oh I would laugh.

Playing with an empty plastic bottle, and lasting for ages.
Until enough was had, he would lay while I read papers.
And on a balmy summer night always etched in my head.
Us, resting on the driveway, his head resting on my leg.

He's memory in my heart, I will hold so close, so near.
As do my family, he was one of us and so dear.
He still is talked about today, and every now and then.
Someone will tell a story, at how he touched them.

I know I can't write all the humorous times in his life.
The fun, the laughter, from myself, Daughters and Wife.
So this is a tribute to him, the memories that won't abate
This bloke that gave unconditional love, our four-legged mate.

LOVING AGAIN

Years now, stuck in this rut, it has been such a strain
Oh! You are my man, making me feel so loved again
From the day I met you, yes I know it's plain to see
The tenderness and passion, that you shower over me.

To describe this feeling one word could surely be sensual
And when you touch me the tingling, so unbelievable
Talking on the phone for hours, well into the night
I know in my heart you're the one, my only Mr. Right.

My body always melts, looking into your eyes so blue
And your Daughters I can love them like mine, it's true
Cause until you, my children were all the love I had
Now I know my future is bright and not all that bad.

So take me in your arms, make this time so arousing
Our lovemaking so intense, strong and overpowering
Hold me now; and together we'll not fade out of sight
Because with you my love, I will spend the rest of my life.

Old Sailor Dan

I'm ushered to his room which stands by the sea
he's watching the ocean while sipping his tea
then with gravelled voice says "come here sit with me"
"this interview, I'm glad the home did agree".

Now shaking my hand I can feel his strong grip
passed me some tea, then I slowly take a sip
deepest blue eyes, brown smoke stained bottom lip
skin like leather, from many an ocean trip.

He views the vast ocean from this patio height
on the wall two lanterns of green and red light
there under the red one, positioned just right
there's an old ship's bell he keeps polished so bright.

Looks out to sea, and knows where he belongs
to ride the waves, his heart forever longs
then at life's end, upon this earth no longer
he will join his mates at Davey Jones's locker.

"I'm the son of a sailor" I'm proud to say
my grandfather sailed to ports far away
he sailed the cold nights or the heat of day
to tropical islands where pretty girls would play.

My father died at sea during world war one
German U-boats on a deadly hunting run
this part of my life now truly came undone
mother disappeared, never to see her Son.

Thankful for those years, my Uncle and Aunt's love
the roof over head, when rains fell from above
calling of the ocean, born into my blood
on a freighter, my sweat's flowing like a flood.

Looks out to sea, and knows where he belongs
to ride the waves, his heart forever longs
then at life's end, upon this earth no longer
he will join his mates at Davey Jones's locker.

Those happy times, a fulfillment in my heart
my love the ocean and I would never part
then 1941 a new merchant ship, a fresh start
Jack telling stories serving on "Cutty Sark".

Then one day the horrors of war came to be
nightmares I wish no generation to see
sunk by "zero's" crew survived, except for three
watching old Jack disappear beneath the sea.

Now Dan sits there, gazing at the horizon
chuckling watching kids, jumping from a pylon
his life was exciting when called upon
He said "It was great when their free time was on".

Looks out to sea, and knows where he belongs
to ride the waves, his heart forever longs
then at life's end, upon this earth no longer
he will join his mates at Davey Jones's locker.

Jamaican Islands where pretty girls would sing
never married, for one girl was not my thing
but one maiden made me feel like settling
my Irish rose, I promised a wedding ring.

My new true love, who could stop my ocean plight
to spend my final days with her in my sight
return to that village, take her as my wife
I lost all contact, almost losing my life.

Son, I spent my life, on the crest of a wave
seen royalty, poverty, saved some slaves
and I lost many friends to an ocean's grave
so now I pass to you my memoirs to save.

Looks out to sea, and knows where he belongs
to ride the waves, his heart forever longs
then at life's end, upon this earth no longer
he will join his mates at Davey Jones's locker.

Months have now passed, I still think of old Dan
I wrote the life journey of this humble man
t'was not his story drawing me to this land
or the deep proud feeling when shaking his hand.

Never told him of my father passing away
nor what I found in his attic the next day
my grandmother's picture with faded bouquet
she wrote "Dan, for your safety and love I pray."

I cried at Dan's funeral, held by the sea
knowing for him, nowhere else he'd rather be
joining Dad and Grand mum, together as three
and finding my Granddad was closure for me.

Looks out to sea, and knows where he belongs
to ride the waves, his heart forever longs
then at life's end, upon this earth no longer
he will join his mates at Davey Jones's locker.

Photo by Ian Stehbens   ceo@peacebuilders.in

Cracker Night

I want to tell a story so let me set the scene
T'was some time ago, before "the chasers" and their team
My brother, mate and myself were often called larrikins
Playing pranks and jokes, sometimes copping some "shellackings"

For weeks, went the planning selling papers for some cash
Buying all manner of crackers, then hiding our secret stash
From the speedway collecting soft drink bottles for some coin
Then buying some skyrockets, watch sailing into the void

Now as this night bore closer and anticipation grew
We would have to sneak out, meet at a place we all knew
The old church at Rocklea, at the back and underneath a tad
Were all our fireworks, almost filling the old sugar bag

Cracker night was here, the smell of sulphur in the air
The cat and dog have gone, cowering under a bed somewhere
Mum was a softie, with her we could get away with anything
Asking "Can we go to Larry's and let some off with him?"

Asking while dad wasn't near or the reply would be "No!"
But mum softly saying "Don't be long boys, now off you go"
So go we did, us good boys never involved in any scheming
If you believed that last line you surely must be dreaming

Rendezvousing at the old church, retrieving our treasured sack
Stuffing our pockets and with the bag slung over Larry's back
The three of us heading off like adventurers into the night
Oh! Yes, this surely would have been a worrying sight

Now Mr. Jackson's place, his letter box a replica of his house
Where a devious plan was hatched, I snuck over quiet as a mouse
Placing inside 4 taped "thunders" with an extra long wick
Giggling a few metres away, expecting the roof to lift just a bit

Well!! Our ears are ringing and with the smoke dissipating
This was a touch more than we were anticipating
Colour drained from our faces so up the road we did bolt
Mr. Jackson standing next to the post, swearing "I'll get you lot!"

Hearts pounding and body's shaking from this awful fright
Running to the railway tracks on this unforgettable night
Making a pact not to blow nice letter boxes into the air
Instead make sure to pick one in need of dire repair

My brother jumps excitingly saying "I know where's one!"
Grabs the bag and starts walking gesturing as to come
There it was, out front of this big house on stilts
Surely to blow this one won't leave us with the guilt's

Oh! What a wreck it was loose, dented and rusted
We would be doing them a favour, shouldn't get busted
All was quiet no lights were on, no one about
So the three of us decided to help them out

In went the "thunders" again and wick well primed
Us waiting on the other side of the road this time
The explosion echoed the night, left there now a rusted stand
Lights came on, voices heard, once again up the road we ran

Walking along a side road and thinking this was quite neat
When around the corner a car slides making a big screech
Fearing the worst I stash our bag and we empty our pockets
The car stops and out flies an angry Mr. Roberts

A huge truck driving man with a temper, I've been told
Pinning us against a wall, in fear I felt my blood run cold
"Please don't hurt us," I said, "we're only having fun"
"Your old letter box looked like it was on its last run"

"It's not the box that bothered me" as he lowered his hand
"I thought, this is it my last breath here on this land"
"Boys, think what could have been", and me just as much a fool
For under my house 2 days ago, stored 7 large drums of fuel

So driving away in the darkness he gives a couple of 'toots'
We're still frozen against the wall, shaking in our boots
Then retrieving our crackers and stowing them in our bag
Deciding our cracker night is over, for this we are so glad

A few days later, behind the old church we make a pact
Never to blow up a letterbox, we just won't do that
Plenty of other pranks to do like changing a street sign
But to you all my friends, that's another story, another time

When Autumn Comes Again

Breezes blow, your free spirits' in the air
Today won't be easy, as my thoughts turn to despair
This goodbye, how it will be such a mental strain
When Autumn comes again.

Thousands of leaves gently falling to the ground
Trudging through dragging my feet, not making a sound
Why is this day so hard, so tough, such a drain
When Autumn comes again.

Clouds overhead becoming so thick and so grey
Blue disappearing as darkness continues on its way
Trying to cover from the cold, seems only in vain
When Autumn comes again.

That cancerous disease came and took you from our life
Always in our minds, Mother, Aunty, partner, wife
Our friends know of, but they can never feel our pain
When Autumn comes again.

No more cuddling on the sofa by the fire warm
Snuggling in each others arms, till the early morn
Wondering about my life, is there anything to gain
When Autumn comes again.

I come to you this day; I leave flowers and a card
Future seasons now without you, will it be hard?
The state I'm in now, wondering if I will stay sane
When Autumn comes again.

Service will be nice; words spoken will be so sweet
Only place now I can hold you is deep in my sleep
In all the seasons your memories will vividly remain
Never more so,
When Autumn comes again.

In memory of our cousin Vicki, 50 years young,
passed away 11/10/2007 a victim of cancer.

RIP

ASA Publishing Company

Photo by Jo Polglase
email : jopolglase@hotmail.com

Rainforest Dreaming

Imagine the beauty, standing in the rainforest, no one else around
To mingle with the animals, not afraid of your sight or sound
With melaleuca's, eucalyptus, burrawang palm and elkhorn abound
The rare rainforest skink stops to look as it scoots along the ground.

Now leaning against a tall northern silky oak, I settle where I sit
In a nearby giant quondon tree a grey headed robin does flit
Singing its monotonous piping whistle, I'm enjoying every single bit
A macleays honeyeater joins the chorus with its "to-wit-to weee-twit".

Shaded by an ivory curl tree a lesser sooty owl trills a squeal
So a rare masked white rat happily enjoys its insect meal
Now looking high into the canopy, this feeling is so surreal
The feeling of contentment and inner peace, one can finally reveal.

Above me a golden bower bird voices a series of rattles and croaks
Then high in a kauri pine ground ward a mahogany glider gently floats
A booming rainforest tree frog, his large air sacks he bloats
There's a bennets tree kangaroo, a young in her pouch she softly strokes.

Some brahminy kites circle atop of the canopy looking for a feed
Next to me a brush-tailed phascogale is munching on a centipede
Lovely pale yellow robins dart about the floor, pecking at some seeds
Two rusty monitors argue whilst rustling in the dead leaves.

Victoria's rifle birds "rasping yaas" add to the forest screaming
To know and name all our flora and fauna would be the best feeling
Wakening to the sound of heavy rain and now it's really teeming
Realizing that once again in my sleep, I was just……….

RAINFOREST DREAMING.

The Surfer

Sitting a fair way off the shore, on a piece of foam and fiberglass
patiently waiting as one swell comes, then watches another pass
the ocean water here is so clear, the creatures, so wonderous
while closer to the shore the sound of the waves are thunderous.

Splashing some water over his face, this feels so refreshing
plying his trade to an art, for years many have been expressing
his adrenaline now quickening, noticing the distance a large swell
he thinks, will this be that perfect ride, that for years they will tell.

Being lifted by this monster now his heart must be pumping
he prays, please don't wipe out here; I'll truly cop a thumping
crouching ever closer to the board as this wave starts to curl
we're watching from the shore, waiting for this scene to unfurl.

Shot out from this liquid prison with a strong blast of spray
heading towards the base of this giant, going all the way
turning and now at the waves centre, this ride seems unending
picking up speed, now towards the top this rider is ascending.

Skimming across the lip, now turn and drop to the other side
we're all clapping and cheering, he paddles out for another ride
staying out there as long as possible until the day's end
once again to ride the surf, another day he will spend.

What is this attraction, riding in heat, cold, wind and the rains?
some say it's the salt water moving through your veins
the feeling of freedom, enjoying the surf, sand and sun
remembering my younger days when having the same fun.

That old Mazda bongo van doing 80 kilometers an hour flat stack
loaded to the hilt with our gear, guitars and boards on the rack
traveling the coast road, finding a good swell, we'd drop in
good friends us four Chris, Blacky, me and a bloke called Darwin.

Now days watching the young doing their lip rides and 360's
reminiscing at what we used to do back then in the 70's
coming here often to watch them, each day is such a treat
content now to sit here in awe as the surf washes over my feet.

Photo by David J Delaney

Storm

Moisture in the air
Humidity stifling
Animals' skit in despair
Knowing and hiding

Light rain now falling
This heat so oppressive
Storm birds stop calling
Darkness so progressive

Wind blowing stronger
Rain heavy and swirling
Staying out no longer
Inside, sounds of whirling

Distant rumbling closer
Lightning lights the sky
Perfect time for a muser
Into the darkness I pry

Trees bending almost breaking
Leaves shredded by stinging rain
Weak branches start snapping
Living foliage feels pain

Flash of white blinding
Earth vibrates shudders
Natures show mesmerizing
Recorded by Philosophers

Through gauze, eerie screaming
Wires touch, spark brilliant blue
Dog in the corner cowering
Is it over, has it passed through?

Rain eases, now a misty shower
Winds gone, trees standing firm
Lightning and thunder, its power
Over the sea, till another return

Moisture in the air
Humidity stifling
Animals' skit here and there
Birds, chirping, flying

Light rain again falling
This heat so oppressive
Storm birds begin calling
Darkness, now regressive.

Winner for the month of December 2007, awarded by "The Creative pen" worldwide poetry web site.

I love writing

I love writing about forests, beaches and sun
Battlers, moms, daughters, dads and sons
I love writing about our brave Diggers present and past
Happy knowing my writings will be read and forever last.

I love writing, watching the awe on a young child's face
Listening as I transport them to their secret place
I love writing, adults mesmerized by a related story
Touching their heart whilst they relive a past glory

I love writing about the outback, heartbreak and pain
My family and the love I know will never wane
I love writing about loving our four-legged mate
Getting it wrong, starting again with a clean slate

I love writing about friends I have met over time
Those that passed on, still remembered in rhyme
I love writing about our wondrous animals and trees
Original custodians of our great land, the Aborigines

I love writing, not worried pleasing experts I meet
Knowing at times I miss the metre, rhythm and beat
I love writing, like other writers all over Australia
Anyone who writes should not be labeled a failure

I love writing, though not good with spelling and exclamation
But isn't it people like us who helped forge our great nation?
I love writing, the contentment and feeling so exciting
I now tell all, I love writing, cause, I love writing.

No Worries

Gentle waves bubbling over my toes
Leaning back a soft breeze blows
In my beach chair, no worries, it shows
Gentle waves bubbling over my toes.

Old Pandanus Tree

*Grand old Pandanus tree
Sentry watching over the sea
Many years have you been with me
Oh! Grand old Pandanus tree*

I am earth my nutrients are so right
Growing stronger with our mother sunlight
Drinking her rays, these days so bright
Sleep gently in the calmness of night.

Remember friend the landscapes changing
Grass trees rejuvenate after a fires raging
New growth after natures raining
Day to night we gracefully keep ageing.

Watching the coming of the first Aborigines
They'd hunt and gather only for their needs
Learnt how to nourish, eating certain seeds
Thank full of the land and air he breaths.

The arrival of "whites" from distant oceans
Planning, these men with grand notions
Scarring the ground and showing no emotions
Praising each other and their self promotions.

Now living in cities choked with smog
Cowering in a room like a frightened dog
Beautiful forests all now but logged
All that's left, surrounded by a putrid bog.

Friend there's hope, a message we can send
There are those, for us they will defend
Stop the destruction bring it to an end
Replant, nurture and let my soul mend.

Learning, together they will make a stand
Once again all the forests will be grand
Landscapes no longer shall be bland
Again, to play together in the clean sand.

Grand old Pandanus tree
Sentry watching over the sea
Many years have you been with me
Oh! Grand old Pandanus tree

Winner for the month of January 2008, awarded by "The Creative pen" worldwide poetry web site.

2008

ASA Publishing Company

Six Feet Tall

Sitting on those cold cement steps,
Waiting to be called, think I'm up next
Patiently doodling as life goes by,
Watching the twirling candy, I let out a sigh.

Homemade singlet, stubbie shorts and bare feet
Coming here, I always thought quite neat
Dad's now finished, I'm called in
"Morning David!" says Mr. Gray as I grin.

Aromas in this shop, one can never forget
No lace, perfumes or girlie hairnets,
A real mans place. They'd laugh, smoke and swear
If a lady did "drop in" they were gentlemen beyond compare.

Walls dotted with photos of horses and footy greats
Dad said, "One could place a bet with Mr. Grays mate"
Huge red leather chairs made you feel like a king,
Collections of hair in the corner, ready for the bin.

Checkered sheet around me, paper towel tucked tight
Sitting like this, must have been a funny site
Mr. Gray says, "David you need a shave it seems"
Dad smiled, nods, to this he jokingly agrees.

Other men present seem to think this is true
Mr. Gray mixed some white, moist, fluffy goo,
With cup, brush and towel he's moving at pace,
Now brushes the mixture all over my face.

Placing fingers firm tilts my head to one side
Down my face I feel the cutthroat blade slide,
Head leaning back, the blade moves up my chin
Mr. Gray looked in my eyes, gave a reassuring grin.

New electric clippers tickled the back of my neck
I asked, "Are you nearly finished?" he said "Not quite yet"
Dusting me off with that wide soft brush,
Now the men are clapping, this did make me blush.

To be a young man among men was a great feeling,
When all shook my hand, this left my mind reeling
Was one of those days a young man could never forget,
Men in a barber shop, laughing, talking or reading a gazette.

There was a strut in my step as I moved across the floor
This kind of feeling, I'd never had before
Turning then waving goodbye to all,
An eight-year-old boy, feeling six feet tall.

Submitted and accepted for publication in "The Curious Record" edition # 21 a N.S.W. magazine distributed world wide.

Voices

Electric activity, in dark corridors
racing deep within my mind,
knowing I shouldn't do this.

Echoing Voices say, Do it! Do it!

Sweat, oozing from my forehead,
vessels pumping, pushing blood through veins,
heated brain feels like exploding.

Haunting voices say, Do it! Do it!

Moving forward, every muscle straining
can't stop what's started, must be finished,
satisfaction must be finally achieved.

Persistent voices say, Do it! Do it!

Why do I do this? Hurts so much
day in day out, why can't I stop?
Thinking of those who need me.

Amplified voices say, Do it! Do it!

WHY? WHY? I ask

Why do people need bloody pianos

<pre>
                    S
                  R
                I
              A
            T
          S
        P
      U
</pre>

Photo by Ian Stehbens ceo@peacebuilders.in

Cycle

Nights reign, almost over.

Golden rays,
creeping over land,
releasing life from darkness.

Tall trees,
first feel heat.

Warm sun,
reaching crevices damp.

Furry animals - peek from burrows.

Birds - stretch wings.

greeting dawn,
cocooned flowers awake,
blossoming,
colours penetrating foliage.

Myriad of perfumes fill,
misty breezes carry,
tantalizing senses.

Droplets of jewels,
on intricate webs.

Moisture,
thick, trickles, from leaves,
crickets creaking echoes within.

Whipbird,
sounds of cracking branches,
Sticky vines curl along brown trunks.

Flowing water,
on endless journey babbling,
bubbling over mossy rocks.

Forest sounds loud,
reverberating all,

Vibrant life,

mesmerizing,

addictive.

Till night reigns again.

Barnawartha

Sunlight breaks through windows, misty from night's cold
kicking off blankets and doona, from this bed so old,
yawning, stretching and scratching my head
moving towards the door, on this carpet of grey and red.

Slowly down this hall, a roadway to the many rooms,
peeking in the bathroom, giggling at uncle, his moe he grooms.
Into the small warm kitchen where family congregates,
while on the old wood stove, a coffee pot percolates.

Flannel jarmy pants hang low and twisted in a bind
ruffled top half tucked in with buttons not aligned.
Nan's mortified, freezing cold, me without shoes
rubbing eyes and grinning, hair sticking up like a cockatoo's.

Yummy hot porridge with honey twirled on top
sitting at the table with granddad, we called him Pop,
finishing brekkie, Nan says, "Need more milk before you go."
Brother and me carrying a billy each, walk toward the road.

Warmed by morning sun we're still in jarmy's, still bare feet,
the dewy grass to road's edge travels parallel with the creek,
we're heading next door, to Roy's small family dairy
knowing we'll have to deal with that old cow Mary.

looking back to Pop's great orchard, fruit glistening in morning sun
Peaches, Plums and Apricots, we'd gouge so many we couldn't run.
Reaching the wooden cattle grid, we're both whistling a rhyme
carefully stepping across four rungs at a time.

Watching for cowpats while moving around the back of the shed,
now comes the part we always used to dread,
Roy said, "For our milk Mary was our cow"
why did he give her to us, that cantankerous old sow?"

I'm pulling while brother's pushing, her head's finally in stocks,
Mum won't be too happy; we're looking like a pair of grots.
Mary's now settled down and I can start the milking,
while we begin to laugh, overhearing Roy's loud belching.

Billies are full; lids tapped on tight.
Releasing Mary, she balks giving us a fright
displaying her usual show of impatience,
reminding us too much treacle creates flatulence.

Ambling towards the orchard that glorious day,
typical boys we splash in the shallows, stopping to play.
No need for the toys that children have now,
we'd climb some trees, eat fruit, chase a cow.

Lying in tall grass staring into the deep blue sky,
watching eagles and hawks while dreaming I could fly.
Nan's homemade pudding with flowing honey icing,
wood stove meals, roast veggies so enticing!

Writing small samples of my childhood life,
knowing I was guilty of also creating some strife.
Now older, I smile remembering the field's sweet fragrance,
as time will never erase, memories of childhood innocence.

Closet Writer

In these modern days of political correctness
uneducated writers wallowing in helplessness
secretly yearning for their work to be recognized
instead, believing they would only be chastised.

Would love their writing to be announced
though some of their words are hard to pronounce
they become "closet" writers of poetry and stories
hiding talents, written from life and memories.

Mostly from early times gone by
schooling wasn't pushed; you'd play footy, kick a try
lived life, didn't worry about what was new
wag school, n' go creek fishing with Blue.

Love writing of lush trees or our land so browned
the Aussie bush or how our birds fly round
all the animals that live in our vast seas
or the pain a soldier feels whenever he bleeds.

You say computers help if we just look
to some of us it's like chasing a chook
O.K. for you, growing up with these things
we can't grasp keyboards and fancy "wing dings".

Writing by hand might be old fashioned
peaceful, quiet, penned with passion
pictured thoughts from glorious surrounds
no tap-tap, whirring or beeping sounds.

Now a few of those who like to judge
don't know if they carry a long held grudge
because they "put in" those years in classes
proudly displaying high achieving passes.

Knowing one must dot the I & cross the T
but look beyond the spelling, see what you can see
I'm sure a beautiful story will unfold
if you give it a chance to let it be told.

If the educated judges throw my work aside
this may hurt or even dent my pride
I'll retreat to my closet and do what I do
that's loving to write from my heart so true.

Consuming Darkness

Dead leaves wash away with accompanying rain,
winds blow along this dark, lonely lane
Why did I do it, why cause so much pain
I can't go on.

Winter's always the worst time you see,
my life changed that day you left me
Never forget how I drove you to that tragedy
You're always on my mind.

So happy, so in love, totally inseparable,
always laughing, always smiling, always loveable
Supporting me, guiding me, my rock, unmovable
Even rocks crumble.

Started with one drink, gradually becoming more,
you could see this demon eating my very core
I couldn't see the heartache, the worry you bore
Blinded by my need.

Consuming darkness within, I started my abusing,
shocked in the mornings, noticing your bruising
This downward spiral, my life's so confusing
Needing more, can't stop.

Staying with me hoping to see change,
too far gone, this life I could not exchange
Satan's power over me seemed pre-arranged
Falling deeper into darkness.

Losing friends, losing dreams, losing my wife,
bottles of pills, finally you took your life
Crying pain, like my heart's been sliced by a knife
You're gone, you're gone, I'm lost.

Living in this laneway, your memories I keep,
brown paper bag, empty bottle lay at my feet
Fluttering eyelids, hazy mind, body feels weak
Slipping, slipping away.

My treasured love soon we'll be together again,
oozing life, my blood flows toward the drain
Like dead leaves wash away with accompanying rain
Finally to be with you.

I was there

I was there when the police came and with you they did sit,
the look on your pale face, shaking, you couldn't believe it.
I was there when you were visited by our family and friends,
also those who came wanting to make amends.

I was there when everyone was listening, not making a sound,
standing beside you when finally I was lowered into the ground.
I was there watching as the people slowly walked away,
my darling last to leave, as the skies were turning grey.

I was there as you slept with my picture pressed to your heart,
thoughts of living without me, the feeling, tearing you apart.
I was there beside you every time you shed a tear,
wondering how you will survive, now I'm no longer near.

I was there when every week to my headstone you visited,
noticing your long visits, becoming less frequented
I was there, you finding it so hard to pack all my things,
keeping my photo for happy times of remembering.

I was there when that glow and smile returned to your face,
happy a wonderful man will soon be taking my place
I was there sharing with you this excitement in your life,
standing beside you as he asked you to be his wife.

I was there; you kissed my photo then, placed it out of sight,
knowing my presence is nigh! I walk towards the light
I was there one last time the memory of your perfume in the air,
just once wishing to let you know, **I was always there.**

*July 2008 2nd place winner
ASA Publishing Company poetry competition.*

ASA Publishing Company

Untitled Love

In decadent days of times long past
when secret passions were publicly outcast,
comes forth a story of love unbridled,
a scene, forever to remain untitled.

Unburdened he travels a free new world
unknowing the events to be unfurled.
A handsome man, soft curly hair of black,
impeccably dressed, though with battered hat.

A lady, gold hair and eyes emerald green,
silken dress and bonnet of lace, such beauty unseen.
Married a man, a lawyer refine,
many nights for affection she'd pine.

Two days travel, for her young sisters' birthday,
far from her house now loveless and grey.
Polite conductor their tickets he checks,
bids good evening then moves to the next.

Introduces himself this gentleman of note,
stows his bag, removes his coat,
she admires his buff athletic stature,
loving brown eyes and perfect posture.

Train shunts forward, starting this journey,
he watches as children play on a gurney,
puffs of black smoke now whisk on past,
there're alone, in this compartment of class.

Lacquered red timber brass polished bright,
ornate luggage racks, crystal clear light,
wide leather seats one could stretch and lie,
blinds pulled down, so others can't pry.

Knowing that life is passing her by,
staring into darkness, she starts to cry,
placing his hand upon her shoulder,
with gentle voice begins to console her.

She tells of a life emotionally starved,
a stage career she could have carved,
instead she married a tyrant of a man,
who rules her mind with force of hand.

He says "My dear, please don't frown"
"Let not your tears, stain your gown"
A trusting smile replaces her tears,
for a moment forgetting her terrible fears.

Trains' gentle rocking brings them closer,
safe in strong arms away from her abuser,
feeling his breath, releases restrictions,
kindled passion overrides convictions.

Smell of perfume, his adrenalin's pumping,
kissing her ear, her hearts' now thumping,
inviting red lips they're soft as velvet,
knowing this night will be their secret.

Heated bodies now moving in unison,
releasing their souls from internal prison.
Tabooed old thoughts finally dismembered,
forbidden love forever remembered.

Locked embrace under blankets warm,
knowing they'll part, with coming of dawn,
unstoppable love they knew at first site,
memories now, this indelible night.

He walks from the train, stops then turns,
now on the platform this man her heart yearns,
tips his hat as the carriage moves slowly away,
hoping their paths may cross again some day.

Received the estate when her ill husband died,
time has passed, to herself she does confide.
Remembering that night, her thoughts drift back,
then watches her son, soft curly hair of black.

Crying Souls

Lurking, lurking mist creeping round headstones
Moistened soil covering decaying bones
Lurking, lurking mist.

Swirling, swirling through grasses and crosses
Zephyrs brush across thickly green mosses
Swirling, swirling zephyrs.

Hanging, hanging moist vines draping from trees
Rhythmic swaying with the flowing gentle breeze
Hanging, hanging vines.

Chiming, chiming town clock striking midnight
Eeriness overcomes this old graveyard site
Chiming, chiming, striking.

Rising, rising souls their nightly journey
Trapped within for their eternity
Rising, rising souls.

Glowing, glowing contorted bodies seen
Silver moonlight enhances gothic scene
Glowing, glowing bodies.

Floating, floating ghostly figures that cry
Skeletal, decaying flesh, sunken eyes
Floating, floating ghosts.

Screaming, screaming voices reliving pain
Blood upon blood washed away with rain
Screaming, screaming voices.

Returning, returning toward their grave
Forever they will remain Satan's slave
Returning to Satan.

Approaching, approaching dawn brings forth life
Serenity instead of ghoulish strife
Approaching of the dawn.

He lives in the tropics

He lives in the tropics
wasn't always so
far from troubled life
of so long ago.

Kick out of home
living in "shooters pit"
often selling his body
just to get his "hit".

Remembers darkness
addicted to a syringe
dying in a gutter
overdosed heroin binge.

Hospital Chaplin reads last rights
views his body from above
an angel gives him hope
return and spread his love.

Released from rehab
remembers that promise he'll keep
away from gutters of death
where demons taunt and creep.

Loves balmy nights
under swaying palm trees
smell of salt air
cooling gentle breeze.

Plays guitar to tourists
they drop coins in his case
chats to the locals
tells, how he loves this place.

Zephyrs swirl night air
he continues singing songs
on this tropical evening
moonbeams through palm fronds.

He lives in the tropics
wasn't always so
a heart full of love
shares with all as they go.

2009

ASA Publishing Company

Night Mistress

Eyes feeling heavy, still there's no reprieve
As every K draws me closer to my goal.
Thinking of my family, I start to grieve:
This mistress of night has taken my soul.

Bull lights shine, piercing the dark abyss,
Illuminated eyes glint in fear;
How many, I wonder become a near miss—
Dart into the scrub then disappear?

ZZ Top blast their tune to no avail,
My head's ever cloudy on this chilly night.
Fresh cool air I deeply inhale,
Hoping back home, everything's right.

My wife once again is sleeping alone,
I know she wishes I'd give it away;
Fearing the worst from the ringing phone,
Strength and bravery must be displayed.

White flash startles me from a trance—
Was this owl an omen, a greater spirit's will?
Through the darkness I continue my advance,
Remembering, micro-sleeps kill.

Mirrors reflect an untraceable past,
Clearance lights snake into the distance;
Windscreen highlights the future so vast,
This old rig shows no resistance.

Now at a truck stop, far from family and home,
Glad my night mistress for the moment has gone.
Why do I do this? The answer remains unknown;
I'll keep driving, I'll continue on.

I was the only Queenslander selected from hundreds of submissions and was flown to Sydney to perform my poem at Olympic park, Sydney, 21st March 2009 for "Dust poems" a project by the Redroom Company, "poetry by Australian Truck drivers".

Male Dilemma

Approaching now with trepidation
Heart thumping anticipation
Brow soaked in perspiration
Throat tightening asphyxiation.

Echoed voices, feeling fearful
Clouded mind now in freefall
Transfixed eyes becoming tearful
How can she be quite so cheerful?

Just in there! She softly motions
Brain is racing with emotions
Scented whiff from bottled lotions
Perfumed aroma drifts from potions.

Trembling hands begin to reach
Wishing I was at the beach
Sacred law, I'm about to breach
Remembering, what Dad did preach.

I can't do it, collapse in beanbag
Feeling like a rung out dishrag
To all you men, keep reading a mag
Never, delve into a woman's handbag.

Photo Mick O'Brien outside the ruins of his property

Black Weekend 2009

Along the mountain side they grow
as their flames rage through th'small shires
Then down the valleys and plains they blow
do these wild unchallenged killer fires.

With red hot embers from above
no chance to out run its advance
Knows naught of compassion nor of love
as it taunts with its orange flame dance.

Now leaves behind a landscape charred
with debris choking many brooks
Survivors now forever are scarred
from the terror when hiding in nooks.

So many homes, razed to the ground
possessions are gone in a flash
there's heartache and sadness all around
now begins the sifting through the ash.

We watched horrific T.V. scenes
like Satan had returned with hell
he pushed destruction to extremes
now leaving a charred, pungent smell.

They're saved from blackened barren land
our fauna subdued by their burns
Koala drinks from a fiery's bare hand
help's needed till the bush re-turns.

To Fiery's, their lasting dogged strength
continued their fight till the end
Your selfless acts taken to any length
though losing many neighbours or friends.

They will return, stand proud and tall
determined to stand the tide
they fought with their backs against the wall
it's that famous yet stubborn Aussie pride.

Grand Daughter, Zoe Kinsella.
Photo by Daughter, Lisa Kinsella

Sharing some Tea

She sits alone in the shade of a tree
pretending to sip her own cup of tea
her tutu's so fine and lined with braid
with butterfly wings that nanna made.

A China tea set coloured with flowers
at grandad's table she will play for hours
on chairs for her that were made with love
curious robins watch from above.

Not really alone, her friends are all there
there's Simba the lion and Benny the bear
Molly the dolly dressed refine
Penny the penguin's nursed all the time.

Her milky white skin is so soft and smooth
a ferocious wild beast her voice could soothe
sparkling brown eyes that always shine bright
now having you here is pure delight.

Happily playing, full of innocence
moving about with total eloquence
turning to blow your grandad a kiss
makes me proud my cheeky little Miss.

You ask me to join and share a "hot" drink
approaching the table I give a wink
under this tree our laughter echoes
tickling your feet right under your toes.

Now on my lap and you give a big hug
then plant a kiss on my old bearded mug
I will remember these days with glee
sharing tea in the shade of a tree.

Colours of Cairns

Relaxing on the pier boardwalk
Enjoying a coffee from Piccolino
On the Bigcats people board
Then across the blue ocean they go.

Blue-ish distant mountain ranges
A back drop in azure skies
Lush green rainforests
Where the rainbow Lorikeet flies.

Visual beauty of the Great Barrier Reef
Endless walks along golden sand
Crystal droplets sparkle in morning sun
Ulysses butterfly, their brilliance so grand.

There are always the colours of Cairns
Like red sunsets full of splendour
Fond memories are now embedded
Of your far north's great adventure.

Gone

I cry my child; you're wrenched now from my heart
taken away, we're forever apart
the church white collar men say it's the way
no longer your life, you have no say.

I cry my child, now stolen from our clan
locked away you're now an angry young man
beaten and whipped to follow white man's rule
now forced to believe you are a fool.

I cry my child, for you, I'll never hold
I'll never forget you when growing old
and miss you when roaming throughout our land
walking creek beds or the desert sand.

I cry my child; these men seek our women
they shave their head, then work them like stockmen
they're taken from their ancient way of life
bed with white man, never called a wife.

I cry for my land, old ways disappeared
Gone is the lifestyle when my food was speared
Gone is the hope, traditions of our land
Gone is the time, we, were proud and grand.

My Poetry

For farmers toiling fertile land
working hours with calloused hand
overcoming life's adversity
providing for humanity
For you — I write my poetry.

For those who live in our small towns
surviving seasons, greens or browns
fire, floods or droughts existence
learning from your own persistence
For you — I write my poetry.

For city folk who like bright lights
the traffic, smog, historic sights
lanes that house poor and needy
the rich bankers fat and greedy
For you   I write my poetry.

Young soldiers fault and gave their lives
leave behind family and wives
so many died unnecessarily
our freedom from your bravery
For you — I write my poetry.

Those holding to their seats of power
playing politics hour after hour
forgetting people amongst bureaucracy
we'll remember your accountability
For you — I write my poetry.

For learned scholars of highest reverence
teaching young literary ebullience
some forget the power of simplicity
in rhyming stories and all their beauty
For you — I write my poetry.

With smiles or tears full of contentment
feelings of unwavering commitment
the scribe pens line so diligently
One, understands the written complexity
For me — I write my poetry.

Monster Crack

Living a wonderful, normal life
Employment, home, family and wife
Who'd predict this downhill trend?
Into a world, one can't comprehend.

Doesn't care what family set
High school grad. Or Air force vet.
Once you play the game my friend
A downward spiral, you quickly descend.

All it took was just one 'pull'
The feeling now, is irresistible
To another state I flee
But the demons always follow me.

I'm living in this dingy lane
Picking up butts from the drain
Thieving, scheming to buy a 'brick'
Selling my soul to get my hit.

Ever wary of all you meet
Searching for 'crack' upon the street
Eating scraps from local bins
Thinking naught of all my sins.

Lying in my cardboard box
Wishing I could stay the detox
Clasping tight this stem of glass
Watch as other users pass.

Another haunting night approaches
In this laneway full of roaches
Demons start their nightly game
Toying with my life of shame.

Smoke another piece of 'crack
Knowing there's no turning back
Now I play the game so well
Living my own private hell.

Second spell I've spent in jail
When released I must curtail
This monster that's been in control
Take back from it my very soul.

Now I'm President of ASA
A publishing company in U.S.A.
Supporting writers, local or worldwide
Survived a life where I should have died.

Dedicated to Steven Lawrence Hill,
President of ASA Publishing Company, Author, and friend.

Will there be Peace?

Why does the human race, destroy their fellow man,
change a way of life, take control of someone's land.
This is the way it's been, all throughout the ages,
written in detailed reference on many historical pages.

All religions preached, of loving one another,
join with them or die, standing by your brother.
For it was those early years, also sometimes later,
religious wars were fought, human life did not matter.

History has recorded not only religion was the seed,
man is truly guilty of lust, jealousy and greed.
Why must one be better than his neighbour?
show the world your might, rattle the deathly sabre.

Leaders of world nations for one reason or another,
send our young off to war, leave behind a grieving mother.
They say it is for peace, to free our fellow man,
then why do thousands die following their leaders plan.

Wouldn't it be great, to see peace in our lifetime,
I dream we all will live as one, maybe write some rhyme
When the noise of guns and bombs, finally do cease
only then my friends — we will, **hear the sounds of Peace.**

Photo by Bev Delaney

Grandchildren

They rummage in the pantry
they're fighting in the hall
and leave their dirty prints
on every single wall.

There are balls up on the roof
there's shuttlecocks as well
they walk all through the garden
and ring the front door bell.

They unwind garden hoses
then make a puddling mess
we now see why their mother
is always full of stress.

They leave their sticky lollies
anywhere upon the floor
we even found the blighters
stuck half way up a door.

They hate their evening bath time
can't tell them what to do
they always stall and dawdle
until your face is blue.

Oh! boy! and when they're fighting
it's like a great world war
just when you think it's over
they then front up for more.

Sometimes it's quite unbearable
and almost brings forth tears
the high, brain piercing screaming
leave's ringing through your ears.

Now we are loving grandees
and one thing we must say
when all your grandkids visit
you love them more each day.

Photo by Ian Stehbens

Ocean life

Cooling breezes whisper
rustling leaves that talk
weathered trees of history
where crustaceans walk

Crystal ocean rolling
shades of blue or green
vibrant coral colours
paint a living scene

Mother oceans stories
moonlight shadows swell
gentle waves are speaking
hidden tales they tell

Vessels, rocking, thrashing
stronger winds now wail
heaving closer daily
ancient people sail

Virgin sand they're walking
in this morning dew
feasting seafood's freshness
toasting life anew

Photo by Ian Stehbens
ceo@peacebuilders.in

Wild Life Angels

There's a group of people
dedicated carers they are
save and nurse the vulnerable
some bearing many scars.

Devotion's always shown
into the night or heat of day
they work to rehabilitate
with healing done their way.

I know super heroes
who fly around and save mankind
well they don't compare with this mob
no better crew you'll find.

helping native fauna
be they homeless, injured or scared
they are taken to the shelter
where wounds can be repaired.

An agile wallaby
this Joey's barely six months old
taken from its dead mother's pouch
it needs to be consoled.

There's many more accounts
involving cars and trucks or dogs
or night time hunting feral cats
killing endangered frogs.

This dedicated team
Far North's 'Wildlife care and Rescue'
to continue their awesome work
need so much help from you.

Sonnets

ASA Publishing Company

Sonnets

In mid November 2009, for the 1st time in my life I read a number of Shakespeare's sonnets & immediately fell in love with the sonnet form, I then googled what is and how to write a Shakespearean sonnet, spent approximately 30 minutes 'studying' then over 2 days completed my 1st sonnet 'A Paupers Friend' I continued to write another 4 incorporating Australian bush & War related sonnets in Shakespearean form.

My 6th sonnet 'Visions of love lost' was a challenge from a friend to write a 'Francesco Petrarcan' formatted sonnet, so again after help from google I read quite a number of Petrarchan sonnets and after a few re-writes was happy with this Petrarchan formatted poem with the story line based in the Napoleonic era.

To those who have studied Francesco Petrarchan would have learnt his known format of an eight line octave, with the rhyme scheme a b b a a b b a. With the last six lines making up a sestet which may consist of following rhyme schemes: (1) c d d c d d (2) c d e c d e (3) c d c d c d (4) c d d c e e, if you have read a number of his sonnets you would also know he wrote in the format I selected for my poem.

2009

ASA Publishing Company

Sonnet no.1

The Pauper's Friend

Now thou hast mingled with the noble class
but they'd not see in life that I do see,
they hold their feasts', drink from their purest glass,
in finest mansions built beside the sea.
See not the homeless begging on the street,
nor in dark laneways, wet with cold they die.
See not the children sick or with bare feet,
nor for the measly scraps thrown out they vie.
If I could forward through the frames of time
to lands afar unheard of now by thee,
would not thine eyes view pestilence and crime,
would still there be fine mansions by the sea.
Where still are those who sleep in laneways cold,
where nobles, whom for wealth their souls they've sold.

Sonnet no. 2

A Stockman's Passing

He sleeps beneath the trees in battered swag
while cattle doze not far from where he lies.
As other stockmen camp nearby and brag,
this old man loves the quiet, star-lit skies.
He knows his life is nearly at an end,
but once again, his mind drifts back to her.
That past event he still can't comprehend;
the deadly fire to him is still a blur.
For twenty years he's droved the mobs alone,
though with his working mates he's moved along;
Within his mind her ghostly figure's shone,
for twenty years she's sung their wedding song.
A new dawn breaks, but still the old man lies;
Together now they walk beneath clear skies.

Photo by Ian Stehbens   ceo@peacebuilders.in

Sonnet no.3

Snowy Mountain Blood

He views the brumbies fleeing down the hill
while now he's chasing, closing at great pace.
And knowing that one slip out here could kill,
he can't afford a tumble or lose face.
The cracking stockwhip sounded as he cheered
it echoed through the valley far below.
These Queensland mountains many have revered,
though riders died when footings lost would throw.
Remembers how the man rode snowy's side,
his father told the story long ago.
And how his heart beat hard with so much pride,
it was his Granddad dealt the best a blow.
He fronts the mob and halts them with one crack!
now with them all defeated, drives them back.

Sonnet no. 4

Nature and War

Soft morning sun shines through moist droplets clear
now radiating coloured prisms bright.
The almost silent brook is trickling near
as Autumn leaves float to the ground so light.
While pristine beauty now is all abound,
though some short years ago this was not so.
There were no flowers growing from the ground
the trickling gentle brook had ceased to flow.
With soldiers corpses rotting in the mud.
No fields of green, or pollen on the breeze,
just craters with the deads' own flowing blood
that soak the roots of what were once grand trees.
When fighting's done, then nature plies her trade,
as once again the man made horrors fade.

Sonnet no. 5

Why

New morning sun brings forth her warming rays
while dying leaves drift gently to the ground.
Approaching winter soon will dampen days,
when ice will hang from barren trees abound.
Korea's changing beauty I have seen,
penned every scene for all the world to read.
I miss so much your sparkling eyes of green,
while for your love, my heart again will bleed.
The freezing snow will cover all that lives
I hope I will survive this daily fight.
A priest once said that Jesus Christ forgives,
though what I do, he could not see as right.
My helmet sits upon my weary head —
My rifle, now replaces pencil lead.

*For my Uncle, Lawrence George Delaney,
who fought in Korea, RAIC, 1st Battalion, RAR.*

Sonnet no. 6

Visions of Love Lost

My arms outstretched again my dearest love,
I'm watching as your dress glides on the grass,
Your vibrant beauty no one can surpass,
with fragrant skin as soft as Turtle doves.
You lift the bonnet from your hair of red,
then hand in hand we kiss beneath the Yew,
your angel voice speaks of arrangements new,
for soon, as wife you'll share my modest bed.
Your tears of fear they stain your perfect face,
though, to this fight we knew I had to go,
we tremble as we hold each other tight.
Your visions fade now from this barren place,
your loved betrothed dies in cold Russian snow
as Bonaparte, retreats with closing night.

"Embrace every day for what you have
Don't be disillusioned by what you can't have"

David J Delaney ©

ABC Topical poems

ABC Radio 'topical' poetry

In late November 2008 I was proud to be asked to be the ABC Far north radio's first ever poet Laureate writing "topical" poetry on news worthy media reports mostly about the far north of Queensland, but also including some state, national and international news reports.

For this task I was required to write my poem in 4 days, sometimes finishing on the morning I was to read on air, the reaction from ABC staff, public, and the average person on the street was very gratifying.

The following is a collection of my poems which were performed live by me on air at ABC radio studio's Cairns, north Queensland, almost all have not been altered or rewritten in any way and are basically as they were presented on air.

ASA Publishing Company

2008

ASA Publishing Company

Henry and Billy

Now here's a man who could inspire a nation
One so brave and full of inspiration
Descending a tower in our northern city heat
He did this you see, without the use of his feet

A white knuckle descent, our local paper read
Broke his neck diving, that's what they said
Now his legs are replaced by wheels
How many of us would know how this feels

So after a day's work when you whinge and gripe
Think of Henry and his life time plight
I salute this man, his courage and tenacity
To push aside this partial incapacity

And how could I pass up another so bold
For the young will remember as he grows old
He tackles his foe and darts through willy nilly
Deserves all the accolades, yes! That's our Billy

Just goes to show we breed them tough up here
Our sports people prove their worth year after year
He's the king of the north, even Wally would be proud
But Billy would say, Aw! It's nothing and disappear into the crowd

They come and they go

Politicians come and go, spread their party's waffle
To us mere mortals it's often a load of offal
Our pensioner's plight, becomes totally irreverent
While polies complain of portions there're eating in parliament.

When all our polies visit, they should be herded on a bus
Then find out for themselves, why there's such a fuss
They ride around town with an air-conditioned view
Instead of feeling like well done snags on a local barbeque.

Where're about to fight, another cyclone campaign
Our roads will be cut again by continuous driving rain
We all know our members are there for number one
When all we want is for something to be bloody well done.

The so called weather guru's are predicting the worst
Their well meaning message is precise and well versed
Believe them or not, we really should prepare
Removing dangerous objects that could fly through the air.

Some hope Baz's *"Australia"* will stop the tourist slump
And the increase in visitors, quickly it'll jump
Already around town if you listen to the chat
Tourists are snapping up our famous Akubra hat.

The Kiwi's won league's cup, yes this is true
I'll graciously give credit where credit is due
But while you Parrrrrty, don't spruik to loud my chum
Just remember we've won nine to your lonely one.

It's just not Christmas cheer

So 600 jobs equals one percent, now I don't mean to offend
But I don't class half a percent as insignificant my friend
Though you did show concern and no malice was meant
See, these are real people, not a number or percent.

Fanatics kill tourists in the city of Mumbai
When will the bleeding hearts stop turning a blind eye?
Terrorism is murder and really should desist
They should be stood against a wall, not a smack on the wrist.

When will we get polies with some genuine foresight?
Where on a major rail crossing there's just a flashing light
Blind Freddy could see problems would be increased
How do they sleep at night, thinking of the deceased?

It's that time of year, our swimming holes are flowing
Heavy rains and thunder storms get those rapids growing
Can't understand why anyone would risk it
Think I'll stay at home and watch the cricket.

Where has north Queensland's good will gone?
When a family and their bus keep getting moved on
Think of the wonderful stories the children will tell
Can't they live the Aussie dream as well?

Christmas, I'm over it!

You finally sit exhausted with presents wrapped to go
When a voice in your head screams "No oh! No"
How could it happen, forgetting dear Aunty Maude
And that single golf ball just won't suit Uncle Claude

Dreading the thought, knowing the battle will be on
Return to the centre and fight the marauding throng
Then stand in the check out queue, forever once again
Avoiding that amorous boy working in isle number ten

Dashing to the car, feeling our Christmas heat
Instantly start sweating from your head down to your feet
Quickly learn the art of driving with one finger
Steering wheels to hot but you know you can't linger

Now what's that racket coming from under the bonnet
Certainly doesn't sound like a beautiful sonnet
In the middle of the driveway, now at a stop
From the air con. The breeze is pumping red hot

Emerging from that oven, stubbing your toe on the gutter
Wanting to scream, but all you can do is mutter
Limp into the house, soaked through from your sweat
Perched in front of the air con, arms outstretched like an egret

Maude can have a card with forty dollars within
This year she can buy her own bottle of gin
Savouring Bellissimo Gelato as on the lounge you sit
Thinking to yourself, "yep! Christmas I'm over it!"

The have's, have not's and in-betweens

Did I hear right, have I been deceived
Federal politicians really have me peeved
A rumoured $100,000 pay rise, just isn't right
When for $5.00 we have to scream and fight.

Are they really there to feather their own nest?
Do their trips to Disneyland, and stuff the rest
Economic times force us to tighten our belt
Another cruel card to the people will be dealt.

Well I don't know if this is on the back burner
Perhaps it could be explained by our own Mr. Turnour
I know at times it's rather fruitless to say
But! Should they be reminded of who pays their way?

Why is it, those who fight the hardest suffer the most
Liz and Max, your strength and tenacity I truly toast
Fighting bureaucrats is like battling Siberian blizzards
Liz, you're a survivor we know you'll beat both the bastards.

Who cares if Sonny Bill is back on our turf?
The biggest over rated player here on earth
Where are the Aussie's? NRL selectors lack some spleen
And our clubs say my Kiwi team is better than your Kiwi team.

2009

ASA Publishing Company

Aussie pride, Aussie shame

She's our girl once again, is our Jelena
Captured all our hearts right here in Australia
A true inspiration, plus sharing a confession
For years she's been fighting debilitating depression.

I stand by our flag with honour and pride
But what I saw made me cringe and want to hide
If you're a hoon, lout, yobbo or punk
Don't insult our flag wearing it when drunk.

Met Tanya Major just the other day
Proud Kokoberra woman, up Kowanyama way
Dances a mean "Coyote ugly" I hear
Great ambassador, this former young Australian of the year.

How can we fix the worldwide economy?
When Wall Street titans think they have autonomy
Recently paid bonuses worth 18.4 billion
Then they wonder why public anger turns vermilion.

I really thought the Aussies were down, beaten and burned
But then their fighting spirit once again returned
Sure the kiwis beat us, this game they only just won
I thought it was a great finish, them winning by one run.

Could this be the wet season, like the one's of old?
As the rains, wind and cyclones begin to unfold
So why is it so, some complain and whinge every year
It's the tropical far north; please explain why you live here.

Troubled Times

Anyone would think Mother Nature has lost the plot
We're receiving record rains, while down south it's stifling hot
Why all the flooding, it's a mystery to me
While Victoria's fires are now the worst in history.

The dangers that lurk when flooding creeks rise
How muddy waters become the perfect disguise
News filters through and it's really quite a shock
A five year old boy is tragically taken by a croc.

Why do they do it, why take a chance
When approaching flooded roads continue their advance
Don't rely on good luck or good old wishful thinking
Now we have a man drowned and another still missing.

Makes me shake my head and I truly wonder why
How some cause so much grief and make people cry
Seems a lot of Victoria's fires were deliberately lit
Hearing about these low life's, I just couldn't believe it.

I'm a Maroon and I say it with pride
But now is the time to put state rivalry aside
I know they're Mexican's, but they're Aussie's as well
In need of our help to survive their own hell.

Banks and Red Cross are taking help by the score
Let's show how north Queenslander's can come to the fore
We've got our own troubles, yes! I know this is true
But see what you can spare and show you're true blue.

It's the way we do it, Aussie helping Aussie
Banding together is part of our history
Fighting fires, flood or on a distant foreign shore
Our camaraderie leaves other countries in awe.

Promises made, Hope revisited

Once again our supply line was cut
Roads flooded for eight long days or so
Our pollies continue to sit on their butt
Forgetting promises made not long ago.

And it doesn't matter what political persuasion
They'll always blame one 'n other
While every year we live in anticipation
As Brisbane builds tunnels one after another.

Australian's everywhere you've done us proud
The world all over, from backpackers to celebrities
Answering the call for help, so strong and so loud
Donations pour in supporting fellow Aussies.

Let's not forget our mates in western Queensland
Surrounded by flooding the size of South Australia
Helping all Aussies should go hand in hand
Here's hoping support for them won't be a failure.

National parks are deafly quiet on recent tragedies
And green groups seem to have gone to ground
Maybe introduce burn offs, once done by Aborigines
Build firebreaks, remove tinder fuel that's now abound.

Tahlia's beauty spot now has Oprah talking
This sixteen year old of the Kuku Yalangi tribe
Oprah might visit and do some rainforest walking
Aboriginal life, young Tahlia will proudly describe.

Walk against crime was held Sunday morning
With the public, politicians and even ex coppers
If you see a crime, phone and give forewarning
Don't hesitate, ring crime stoppers.

Let's work together

We know the Victorian fires are a shocking tragedy
And the support they've received is simply the best
But our folks here are suffering great adversity
Still surrounded by floodwaters way out west.

And the power boffins, who think they run this state
Eating in restaurants and displaying a lack of compassion
Have the hide to tally, banter and debate
While flooded communities are forced to ration.

Emergency services minister says he didn't know
About the state of our flooded land
He mustn't read or watch the T.V. news show
I think he'll have to remove his head from the sand.

We have been asked to dig deep again
For Saturdays Cowboys v Penrith match
Then at the end of the game we could all say amen
Think of those who have lost their small patch.

What the hell's happening in this wonderful city?
When visiting tourists are raped, robbed or bashed
Our well meaning judges should stop taking pity
As the low life's walk around unabashed.

The police do their best when apprehending
But, then the law is an ass to me
With pin stripe suited lawyer's defending
These animals seem to get off scot free.

I can't believe the warnings go unheeded
With Dengy the worst some have ever known
Our help, scientists have continually pleaded
Cause they can't rid this outbreak alone.

Political promises, Political circus

Here we go again; as they appear from the wood work
Promising and spruiking party rhetoric and waffle
Their wholesome and goodness act makes me irk
With minders in tow, through towns they waddle.

All on offer, their coffers now open
Shaking hands, kissing babies and pretending to listen
Hospitals, roads and schools, their voices will deafen
Be wary of promises that sparkle and glisten.

The battle's on, trying to out do one 'n other
Party faithful slapping each other on the back
With full media coverage our minds they'll smother
Vie for your vote with a full frontal attack.

Now Ms Hanson, she's known throughout Australia
Popping up and running another political campaign
Got some "Ticker" continuing after her last failure
But spare us that old phrase "Could you please explain".

Do you study the form, listen to what they say
Every election I seek that bloke called Gerry Mander
He's always talked about and discussed any time of day
Can't even find him on any ballot paper.

If it wasn't so serious we would all have a good laugh
Throw some sawdust round to complete the circus
Standing in front of their oversized photograph
Mmm!! Is that really them or is it hocus-pocus.

Now I'm by far not a moggie lover
But a horrific event happened on the weekend
A sickening sight the post did uncover
This kind of cruelty unfortunately is becoming a trend.

Bad decisions, Critical consequences

How about this bio security mob
Allowing imported bananas into our county
Public concerns they seem to snob
Makes you wonder if they collect a bounty.

Why aren't our leaders voicing concern?
As our growers struggle to make a quid
This foreign fruit could carry any germ
The risk's too great, they should be prohibited.

Mangoes sell for a king's ransom it seems
The middleman has dollars in his eyes
While, of such riches our farmer dreams
Labouring hard, wondering how he survives.

Our third cyclone and still there's panic buying
Hello! This is the cyclone season
Last minute stocking to me is mystifying
Prepare before, then for panic you'll have no reason.

Footy has started and already a major scandal
In any code they all suffer the same
Seems to me instant fame some can't handle
Surely respect can be brought back into the game.

Decisions have been made on the fate of some pensioners
They'll try to fight the uncaring white collar
Who'll level their home for the sake of developers?
People's lives are traded for the dollar.

Their up in arms, the toffee nosed posse
Cause Kevin let slip and swore
Just shows he's really an Aussie
Some toffee's I find a total bore.

Deadly complacency, proud Muso's

Can you truly believe the audacity of some?
We're still finding water in tyres, boats or a half cut drum
These people are so ignorant at what is really happening
With over six hundred victims, effected, sick and aching.

I'm so gobsmacked at the total complacency
Are they for real or just complete zombies?
Wake up! Think about your vulnerability
Clean up your yard, show some responsibility.

Of late it's been difficult to write a positive story
When media reports of doom, or some murderer's glory
I do know they're out there and I will find some to tell
But as media bosses know, good stories just don't sell.

A damn parochial Queenslander, of this I'm truly proud
When selected to represent us, I'm still walking on a cloud
Me! Performing in Sydney, who ever would have thought?
That my humble poems would be so eagerly sought.

Concerts were held for victims of fire's and the flood
Again, shows the Aussie spirit that's embedded in our blood
Those from the music industry, to you I do salute
Giving pride and hope to those left almost destitute.

In this world of technology, mobile phones and such
There are those, who can't seem to live without their touch
It really irks me, when at the theatre or out dinning
To hear someone talking of their massive pile of ironing.

Sign of the Times

Six of the best holiday spots here in the north
Operators are hoping more tourists will come forth
If we can just keep the lowlifes off the street
Visitors to Cairns will be in for a treat.

A huge new development was given the go ahead
With restaurants, shops and a unit to lay your head
I'm not quite sure how these businesses will survive
When so many around town have taken a dive.

Who's in the news, but our very own defence minister?
Security chiefs are worried there's something more sinister
He's being wined and dined by a wealthy lady from China
I can see comedians everywhere scribing the odd one liner.

Cairns! The last frontier for the drunk driver
Then when caught, scream like the town crier
This title, for Cairns we don't want to see
Don't drive drunk, show some responsibility.

I believe animals currently have more rights than humans
When a couple live a nightmare with little bat demons
There does come a time when culling can help
Now I've done it! Watch the animal lifer's yelp.

It's great to see indigenous leaders speaking out
To be Aboriginal and what it's all about
Here's hoping Desley uses compassion and tact
And doesn't sweep this under the political mat.

Everyone knows it's April the first
When humorous pranks are duly dispersed
Now I'm not one to keep a secret
But, is that an iceberg I see in the inlet.

Mystery, intrigue, heroes and villains

Changing truckies driving hours, pollies are at it again
But to force prescriptive driving, this really is a gem
I'm all for road safety, as long as it's properly set
Restrict the public's driving, see how far you get.

It's hard enough for truckies as is
If you actually leave your office and take a good squiz
Cost of tyres, fuel, axel weights and deadlines
For added pressure, restrictive driving times.

Was intrigued with the interview Fiona did
About the ripper who killed street women then hid
Now the possibility he was an artist of note
Was this another way he could taunt and gloat?

Heroes come in all shapes and sizes
Quite often they're in animal disguises
My hats off to "Totty" a real little mate
Saving her owner from a deathly fate.

Bikie clubs of late have made the news
Let's not all come away with one eyed views
BUACA is a group I'll proudly introduce
Fighting for suffering children of abuse.

A far north party, now I'll support with glee
For those in power, the south is all they see
Yes! Form our own party, we do have the choice
Show them down south we have a strong voice.

Bunnies or Babies

It's come and gone, yes! Another Easter
Tons' of chocolates the shops did administer
I think the true meaning has somewhat faded
Beliefs for commercialism have been traded.

Speaking of Easter and all that's a treat
Staff at Cairns base, were run off their feet
With a baby born, one every three hours
It's a wonder the florist didn't run out of flowers.

Can't believe the audacity of thieves
Hiding in bushes and peering through leaves
Sneak onto the patio of Judy's home
Then nick off with her sentimental gnome.

Who was the bright spark suggesting trams?
Run the north and south tracks of Cairns
The idea of trains has been mooted for years
Government inaction has only brought tears.

Soon we won't be allowed to fish at all
From rivers, inlets, beaches or a sea wall
Certain groups are voicing and stomping their feet
Leaves me wondering what they like to eat.

Idiots are still out there, just don't get the drum
Thinking they were O.K. drinking beer or rum
Read the advice, know what you can drink
If you feel you are over, please stop and think.

Banks cry poor, not able to pass on percentage drop
Well, I've never heard so much crock
They're making money hand over fist
Certainly won't be on my Christmas card list.

www.ingramcontent.com/pod-product-compliance
Lightning Source LLC
Chambersburg PA
CBHW041431300426
44116CB00001B/2